# SWIM LESSONS

# SWIM LESSONS

*Ten Secrets for Making
Any Dream Come True*

**Nick Irons**

Clydesdale
PRESS

*Copyright © 2003 by Nick Irons*

*Copyright © 2019 by Nick Irons*

No part of this book may be used or reproduced
in any manner whatsoever without the express written permission
of Clydesdale Press, LLC
except in the case of quotations in critical articles or book reviews.

THE MAGIC STORE by Paul William / Kenny Ascher
©1979 Jim Henson Productions, Inc. Used By Permission.
All Rights Reserved and Administered by Sony/ATV Music Publishing LLC

Designed by Sharon Thorpe
Book Cover Writing by Susan Kendrick Writing

*For my family of dreamers
Mom, Dad, John, and Andy*

# TABLE OF CONTENTS

INTRODUCTION    1

1. LOFTY DREAMS AT 30,000 FEET    7
   *Discover a Compelling Idea*
      Pay attention to recurring thoughts.
      Find a place to dream.
      Allow yourself to daydream.
      Allow your idea to develop over time.
   Make It Happen: #1.

2. INSPIRING WORDS    23
   *Write Down Your Dream*
      Focus on the big picture.
      Tell those you trust.
      Tell the world.
   Make It Happen: #2.

3. A ROADMAP YOU WON'T HAVE TO FOLD    35
   *Make a Plan*
      Choose a planning style that fits you.
      Set priorities.
      Develop a timeline.
   Make It Happen: #3.

4. THE TIME OF YOUR LIFE  51
   *Have Fun*
   Use laughter to keep you sane.
   Use fun to solve a problem.
   Look for humor in your world.
   Laugh at yourself.
   Make It Happen: #4.

5. A CHANGE OF PACE  75
   *Adjust Your Goals*
   Keep what works; abandon what doesn't.
   String smaller goals together.
   Attach a reward to your goal.
   Make It Happen: #5.

6. I THINK I CAN, I THINK  91
   I CAN, I KNOW I CAN
   *Discover Self-Confidence*
   Draw from past experience.
   Face your biggest fears.
   Go forward with blind faith in yourself.
   Make It Happen: #6.

7. KEEP THE FIRE BURNING  107
   *Find Your Motivation*
   Discover what motivates you.
   Be open to new motivations.
   Tap into the motivation of others.
   Make It Happen: #7.

8. WITH A LITTLE HELP  121
   FROM MY FRIENDS
   *Put Together a Great Team*
   Find others whose strengths complement yours.
   Find those passionate about your dream.
   Allow people to do what they love.
   Celebrate along the way.
   Make It Happen: #8.

9. GO WITH THE FLOW  135
   *Be flexible*
   Go with the flow.
   Change your direction as you learn.
   Open yourself to adventure.
   Take a break from your dream.
   Make It Happen: #9.

10. THAT'S RANDOM!  157
    *Be Creative*
    Think of yourself as creative.
    Think in new ways.
    Let yourself see creative opportunities.
    Make It Happen: #10.

11. RAISE A GLASS  177

    EPILOGUE  185

    ACKNOWLEDGMENTS  189

    APPENDIX
    A. *Making a Dream Come True*  195
    B. *Multiple Sclerosis Web Sites*  200
    C. *The Mississippi River*  201
    D. *Swimming*  203

# INTRODUCTION

*The wind howled. Four-foot waves pounded from all sides. My arms burned and my shoulders ached. I gasped to get a full breath of air. Barges the size of three city blocks towered over me, their giant wakes screaming my way. What had I gotten myself into?*

~

I was twelve when my dad told me he had multiple sclerosis. Over time, I watched as MS stole his ability to walk with ease. Although he did his best to make light of his situation, he would fall and it tore at my heart. I was just a kid and, more than anything, I wanted to slay this dragon…somehow. For over a decade, I asked myself, "What can I do?"

Then on an airplane, 30,000 feet in the air, I looked down at the Mississippi River and realized I didn't have to stand by and watch. The crush of weight I had carried for too long was lifted.

On June 1, 1997, I plunged into the fifty-six degree water of the Mississippi River in Minneapolis, Minnesota, and took the first of more than a million strokes that would propel me down the longest stretch of water in North America.

From the beginning, I was convinced that everyone in America would see me swimming, hear my story, and dig deep into their pockets. Money would pour into the hands of researchers, a cure would be found, and my dad would no longer struggle to walk. With all the idealism of a twenty-five-year-old, I began my journey.

Battling the fury of the River, I thought about quitting...then I thought about my dad. Sheer determination kept me swimming. For 118 days, I stroked through the heartland of America, pulling arm over arm through ten states and countless small towns. Five hours a day, six days a week, immersed in the muddy water, I swam through storms and waves, whirlpools and pollution.

After four long months, I climbed on shore in Baton Rouge, Louisiana, and became only the second person in history to swim more than 1,550 miles down the Mississippi — and the only one to do it with the locks and dams of its "modern" form.

My dad was waiting for me on the bank of the River. My dream was complete. With the invaluable help of my family, we raised tens of thousands of dollars for MS research, and people across the country learned about the disease.

Since then, I have been asked a hundred times, "How did you do it?" An inquirer often adds, "I admire your courage, but I could never do anything like that." I believe anyone can.

When I began planning the Swim, I was a twenty-three year-old recent college grad working in an unfulfilling job 3,000 miles from my family. My life was filled with financial woes; both my electricity and gas had been turned off at one point, and my car had been repossessed.

I had never done any fundraising, PR, or marketing. I had no experience with selling, interviewing with the media, or finding sponsors. I had never seen the Mississippi River up close, and I was a sprint breaststroker, not a distance freestyler. I simply had a dream that touched me to the core and a burning desire to make it come true. I would do whatever it took to make it happen.

With enough passion and excitement, anyone can fulfill a dream. You don't have to be the most talented person in the

## INTRODUCTION

world — or the smartest, most connected, luckiest, strongest, or the richest. Using your unique gifts and talents, you can succeed in making your dream happen.

This book is about dreams — my dream and yours. In it, I'll share funny, touching, and dramatic stories that illustrate ten lessons I learned through planning and completing my Swim down the Mississippi — lessons anyone can apply to their dream. Activities at the end of each chapter, in the Make It Happen section, will help you relate these lessons to your life.

If you have ever dreamed a dream, come with me. I promise to be your cheerleader, coach, friend, and confidant. I hope to touch your heart, offer you some insight, and, most importantly, inspire you to turn your most heartfelt idea into a dream that comes true.

# TEN SECRETS

*Nothing happens unless first a dream.*

CARL SANDBURG

# 1

# LOFTY DREAMS AT 30,000 FEET
*Discover a Compelling Idea*

*A dream begins as an idea that won't leave you alone.
It can come from anywhere, at any time, and surprise you
in curious ways. Infiltrating your thoughts, your idea may
show up once a year, once a week, or once a minute.
Like an insistent child, it refuses to be ignored.*

~

In December 1994, I boarded a red-eye flight and crossed the country from Los Angeles to Washington, D.C. The holidays were approaching. I couldn't wait to see my family. The sky was crystal clear as we climbed to our cruising altitude. I peered out the window into the blackness and watched the lights below. About three hours into the flight, the captain announced, "We're flying over the Mississippi River. Look just off the right side of the plane and you can see it."

I gazed down at the landscape awakening in the morning sun and was captivated by a river that stretched as far as I could see. The rising sun cast a brilliant light on the body of water that glistened below. The River looked so calm from 30,000 feet and yet it seemed all-powerful, as it chose its own path. If it wanted to make an improbable, ninety-degree turn to go north for ten or fifteen miles, it did.

My obsession with water began when I was five. John and Andy, my older and younger brothers, and I, less than four and a half years apart in age, spent hours imitating pro wrestling. Each room of the house became a ring where we practiced headlocks and body slams. To save the expense of furniture repairs and therapy for herself, my mom diverted us to the local swimming pool at the Greens Country Club. John and Andy sometimes took a break from the water to play or eat hamburgers. Not me. I would never waste a precious moment of pool time.

I was hooked. For thirteen years, summertime meant "The Greens." I spent hours doing flips off the diving board in a way that my head would never go under the water — a trick that made me a celebrity at the pool. Later, this fun developed into competitive swimming. At first, I swam for The Greens and for Kerr-McGee (a United States Swimming team), and then for Casady High School, and finally for Boston College. At sixteen, during my summer break, I began lifeguarding. Swimming became a defining part of my childhood and identity.

After college, my passion for water led me to Los Angeles, the perfect place to live, with my own pool, the Pacific Ocean, just minutes away. I landed my first "real" job — in television production, working for *American Gladiators*, the classic game show that pitted ordinary (and brave) contestants against the likes of Laser, Zap, Hawk, and Malibu. Unfortunately, I wasn't one of these gladiators…although I secretly wondered if my 6'3" frame and muscles developed from years of swimming would qualify me for the role.

My official-sounding title was production assistant, an entry-level job in every sense of the word. I ran errands. If I wasn't traversing the L.A. freeways from the NBC Studios to LAX, dropping off a script or picking up a contestant, I was repainting an office or trying to assemble the newest IKEA purchase (which I contend had twenty-six pieces instead of twenty-eight).

It wasn't long before the initial excitement of working in television began to wear off. It became a challenge to convince myself that I wasn't wasting a college education. Was my trip to a storage unit contributing anything to society — or was I spending fifty to sixty hours a week making bad TV?

For two short weeks, I vowed not to think about my job. Christmas, my favorite time of the year, offered me a reprieve. I boarded the American Airlines plane that would bring me to my parents' home in Bethesda, Maryland, for the first time in a year.

As I peered out the window at the Mississippi on that late-night flight, I imagined myself swimming its winding curves — raising arm over arm to stroke past barges and boats. I could feel the cool water against my skin and smell the sweet freshness of the air around me. I swam faster than I ever had, helped by mighty currents pushing me forward. Mesmerized, I strained to follow the brown water as it trailed into the distance. Something was telling me "swim the River."

No one is that crazy.

We landed at National Airport in Washington. In the distance, my parents waited for me at the gate. I spotted my mom standing on tiptoes, straining to find me in the crowd. There's nothing she loves more than spending time with her family. Her smile glowed like a beacon.

As usual, she was impeccably dressed; her clothes matched with the perfection she had learned from her father who had designed custom-tailored suits. For a split second, I saw why people stopped her on the street thinking she was Hillary Clinton. Although taller and thinner, facially the resemblance to the then First Lady was uncanny.

Neither of my parents had changed; both still looked younger than their fifty-some years. At 6', my dad stood above the crowd. I saw his smile, perfectly framed by his always-present salt-and-pepper beard. Only once in my life (when I was eight) had I seen him without a beard. He decided he wanted a new look, so he lathered up and shaved. Even though he was thin, he looked at himself in the mirror, examined his chin — or, should I say, chins (an Irons family feature) — and vowed to be bearded forever.

My dad loves having his kids around to share the things he enjoys: Mexican, Greek, Italian, Thai, and French food, and, once in a while, cheap tequila on the rocks. I knew I would soon hear his hearty laugh and loud sneezes.

As I hurried to hug them, a wave of shock gripped me.

My dad and I have a special relationship. In many ways, we are dramatically different. His analytical mind has served him well as a physician; I loathe details. But ever since I was little, we have always laughed at the same jokes.

We have a strange understanding of each other's mind. As partners playing Pictionary, I can draw two straight lines that intersect at the top and my dad will yell "Eiffel Tower." Right. If the game is Cranium, he can hum completely off key, but I'll know it's "God Bless America." We baffle the rest of the family, but we understand.

Multiple sclerosis has been a part of my dad's life for more than two decades. For the first several years, this neurological disease would come and go in its own unpredictable way, as the textbooks say. His double vision would last for a couple of months, leave and return a year later. Some days his balance was worse than others, causing him to bump into a wall or trip and fall. Periodically, the numbness in his legs spread to his feet, making walking difficult, and then three weeks later, he could feel sensation in his legs again. He never knew each morning what new symptom would appear. He never knew if it would ever leave.

Despite the constant anxiety of an uncertain future, my dad did his best to keep his MS from changing his life or ours. A fun-loving father, he laughed and played with us in the pool, took us on the biggest roller coasters, came to all our swim meets, all our soccer, baseball, and volleyball games. At times, everything seemed so normal that I would forget for several months that anything was wrong. Inevitably, reality hit again when the disease plopped like an elephant into the middle of our lives.

As I arrived from L.A., I saw my dad leaning his weight on a wooden cane. The last few years he had slowed down. His progressive disease had weakened the muscles of his legs permanently, yet he had always walked unassisted.

We hugged and then moved slowly to the baggage claim; the uneven rhythm of the toe of his right shoe lightly scraping the floor punctuated the words we spoke.

"How long have you been using a cane?" I asked.

"A couple of months."

"Are you having more trouble?"

He hesitated. "Not really, I just use it to keep other people from getting too close and accidentally bumping into me." With one eye, he glanced to see if I believed his cover story.

We both knew the truth — he needed it to walk. The disease that I had closed behind some door in my mind now stood and stared me in the face, challenging me to ignore it.

What a difference a year makes. Had I really missed this much of his life? Or was his MS progressing more rapidly? He was losing ground. I felt helpless to do anything about it. I wanted to enjoy our holiday time together, worry-free, so once again I pushed MS as far away as possible.


I love Christmas. Everything about it. I love being with my family. I especially love the lights. I attribute this passion to growing up in Oklahoma City. Drive around any neighborhood in December and you'll see Santa and his reindeer emblazoned on many of the rooftops. Industrious little elves with umbilical cords to their electrical source dot the front yards like pink flamingos in Florida.

I couldn't wait to join my brothers at my parents' home to recreate the lights of childhood and replay our fun times. John is sixteen months older than I am. Andy, three years younger. It's hard to believe we're offspring of the same parents. John's full head of blond wavy hair and fair skin contrasts with my bald spot and darker complexion. Andy is halfway between us in coloring, with brown thick curly hair that expands to twice its size with a bit of humidity. We all inherited our parents' height. John is just over 6'. I'm in the middle at 6'3", and at 6'5", Andy towers over the rest of us.

Our interests span the gamut. John's bookshelves are filled with Tolkein and Orson Scott Card, along with a slew of computer and economics books. *Testing Exogeneity* and *Macroeconomics Study Guide* (both with his name on the front) sit side by side. "For Dummies" is conspicuously missing from the titles of John's books. Andy stocks his shelves with scripts for plays from Suzan-Lori Parks, Edward Albee, and William Shakespeare as well as two of his own works, *Paschal Full Moon* and *Non D*. The *Harry Potter* series stands next to Vonnegut, Robbins, and Mailer. On my dresser, *Why Not Me* by Al Franken and *Yoga for Athletes* are piled on top of books by Tony Robbins and Bill O'Neil and James Earl Jones' autobiography.

While at first glance John appears to be reserved, his witty sense of humor and hidden wild side keep us amused. He emulates Emeril in the kitchen and loves eating gourmet meals with a bottle of fine wine. Andy, the ham in the family, fell in love with the theater before his tenth birthday. Through years of acting, he has developed a certain presence so that when he walks into the room you notice all seventy-seven inches of him.

With everyone together again, my brothers and I opened boxes labeled "Christmas" and framed my parents' roof with multicolored bulbs. We bought a fat tree that claimed a full third of the living room. The Virginia Pine dripped with sap that stuck to my fingers. The familiar scent of Christmas followed me everywhere. Presents wrapped in brown shipping paper with red and green yarn bows, straight out of *Martha Stewart Living*, filled the room.

For two weeks, we lived like our Italian ancestors. We gathered in the kitchen. The smell of hot-spiced cider mixed with the aroma of garlic and onions sautéing in olive oil on the stove. We cooked enormous meals, toasted Merlots, shared stories, and laughed.

With renewed energy, I flew back to L.A. Rays of noontime sun bouncing off the plane guided my eye down to the water. Once again, I watched the Mississippi carve its path through the farms below. Visions of swimming flooded back into my thoughts. So did a picture of my father struggling to walk. The two scenes morphed into an intriguing idea.

By swimming the Mississippi, I could help my dad. People would hear about my journey, learn about MS, and feel moved to fund research. With enough money, a cure wouldn't be far behind.

I opened the *American Way* magazine to the map of the United States and felt my heart pound against my chest. Starting from Minnesota, I traced the River with my finger as it cut this country in half.

But could it be done? Could I do it? Without answering those questions, I let them slip away.

Back in my job working long hours, I had no time or energy to think about swimming — let alone swimming 1,550 miles. It didn't matter. Like an uninvited guest, the idea showed up anyway. In the shower, I heard myself singing like Tina Turner, "rollin' on the river." When I tried to find my next delivery drop on an L.A. map, I flashed back to the path I traced high above the Mississippi. Never consciously bringing it to mind, the idea invaded my life.

"Okay, okay!" I silently screamed.

# LESSON #1
## Discover a compelling idea

To make a dream happen, you must first discover your compelling idea. For me, it was a swim down a winding river. For you, it may be a climb to the top of a mountain, a change in careers, a novel you've always wanted to write, or a fun new relationship.

You can recognize your compelling idea by paying attention to your thoughts, noticing ideas that come up again and again. To stimulate new ideas, go to a special place or engage in a favorite activity where you can dream unencumbered by the outside world. Rekindle your daydreaming skills, another good source of ideas.

Once you find your compelling idea, give it a chance to grow and watch it take on a life of its own.

**Pay attention to recurring thoughts.** *Compelling ideas are the seeds of future dreams. They begin as thoughts that come back to you again and again. Notice these thoughts and jot them down. Your imaginings may one day become the compelling ideas that change your life.*

Think about the thoughts swirling in your mind — so numerous you barely notice. Ideas jump from one to another in random associations. If you're like me, you will be reading the words on this page one minute and wondering about the texture of tofu the next. This morning, driving to my office, a.k.a. a table in the Barnes & Noble café, I made note of what came to mind.

"Wow. I love this song. 'I'm living it up at the Hotel California. Such a lovely place.' I wonder what ever happened to the Eagles. They were so big, and then they fell off the face of the earth. Imagine if you could actually fall off the face of the earth. That would make for one cool extreme sport."

Pay attention to your thoughts. You'll notice a few that keep coming back over and over again — invading your mind and your life. The extreme-sport theme has popped into my head a few times lately. Hmmm...I wonder what that means?

**Find a place to dream.** *A place, a time, or an activity where you can dream unencumbered by the outside world can help you discover your compelling idea. Find someplace where your mind can wander and ideas can capture your attention. It doesn't matter if it's the shower, a yoga class, or a cabin in the mountains. Make sure it's easily available to you, and then visit it often.*

Weather forecasters predicted temperatures in the low fifties on a chilly Los Angeles Saturday in January 1995, just after my holiday trip home. I doubt it ever made it that high. A Southern California winter storm hit with a fury...forty-mile-per-hour winds and rain puddling in the street.

The weather fit my mood perfectly. Gray. Running errands ten hours a day, for a job I didn't care about, seemed unbearable. I was plagued by money woes due in part to a monthly car-insurance payment that was more than half my rent (the bane of a twenty-three-year-old, unmarried, male driver living in Hollywood).

There was one upside to the storm. While this intruder brought a wet wind, it also delivered waves that would excite the best surfers. I headed to Manhattan Beach just north of the pier.

I sat in my car, heater cranked up to "Surface of the Sun," watching the angry ocean. Two surfers made it past the surf line to brave the seven-foot waves. Too good to resist. I grabbed my goggles, fins, wetsuit, and body board and ran through the rain to the shoreline. After donning my equipment, I tested the water with my foot, shivered, and jumped in anyway.

I stroked out thirty yards before diving under to avoid a wave crashing toward me. Too late. The moving wall of water shoved me to the bottom. I swam as hard as I could, but tumbling in the world's largest washing machine, I couldn't tell which direction was up. By the time I realized what was happening, I was lying on shore, dazed and confused.

Trying to regain my senses, I looked out to sea and watched a surfer ride one of the largest waves I had ever seen. That's where I wanted to be. The trick was getting out there — past the line where the waves would break — to the water beyond.

I ran into the surf and started over. Swim, dive…BAM! Swim, dive…BAM! Swim, dive…and forty-five minutes later, success. Exhilarated and exhausted, I collapsed on my board in the quieter water sixty yards offshore. I lay back to recover and looked up at the sky before riding the waves I had worked so hard to reach. Pelted by cold rain and physically humbled, I felt so small.

As I contemplated my place in the universe, the ocean quieted my mind. In the throes of this exquisite work of nature, there was no place for negativity or worries about work or money. Only peace and happiness.

The ocean became my escape. It was my refuge, the place I could go, every weekend, to have fun and make life decisions. I played in an enchanted world. Like the dolphins that often swam with me, my mind wandered free. I found my place to dream — big dreams, universal dreams.

**Allow yourself to daydream.** *Daydreaming allows you to think "impossible" thoughts. Don't worry if you didn't survive childhood unscathed by adults who insisted that daydreaming is a waste of time. It's never too late to rekindle your skills. Let yourself be a kid again. You may uncover an idea too compelling to resist.*

Think back to when you were little as you raced miniature cars around a speedway, built a castle in the sand, or read your favorite book. What unknown worlds did you explore?

Daydreaming is an opportunity to visit new places or test new ideas — ahead of time — with no risk. You can wander down paths normally too scary to take or try out experiences often unavailable to you in "real life."

Kids, the expert daydreamers, know that nothing is impossible. If you were a ballerina swirling on her toes, a basketball player with a perfect dunk, or an astronaut walking on Mars, I bet you imagined all the possibilities. So what if you had no money, training, or talent? You saw yourself as a star.

In my favorite daydream when I was younger, I drove the Budweiser sleigh made famous by the Christmas commercial. In the TV version, eight horses prance to the sound of the Budweiser theme song. Thirty-two furry feet keeping time with the music.

Not my team. My Clydesdales galloped. I flew through the countryside gripping the reins with all my might. The wind blew through my then-thick hair as I maneuvered these extraordinary animals with finesse.

Now when I see the Budweiser Christmas commercial, I smile. Secretly, I haven't given up hope. Someday my Clydesdales and I will gallop through the snowy countryside.

**Allow your idea to develop over time.** *A compelling idea takes time to grow — a month, a year, or a lifetime. Be patient while it gradually evolves and defines itself into a dream. When you feel a burning desire to make it happen, it's time to begin. At this point, your dream becomes unstoppable.*

For months after flying over the Mississippi River, thoughts of swimming filled my mind. I was tempted to brush them aside. Little by little, I gave in, deciding to see where they would lead.

I began picturing the breathtaking scenery lining the banks of the River — giant willows swaying in the summer breeze, seventy-five degree days, and blue water so clear I could watch schools of fish swimming by my side, eagles soaring aimlessly overhead.

My dream developed over months. Each time it came back to me, it became a little more defined. I added barges, pleasure boaters, and supporters lining the shore waving and shouting, "Go, Nick! You can do it!"

My snapshot may not have been accurate — there is NO crystal-clear, blue water in the Mississippi and the weather is not always a perfect seventy-five degrees — but it kept my idea alive. When the time was right I made the next move.

## MAKE IT HAPPEN

LESSON #1: *Discover a compelling idea.*

Is there an idea that just won't leave you alone? Is there something you would like to do, become, or accomplish?

Complete the following activities to help you answer these questions.

1. Finish these sentences:
   - *If I had all the money in the world, I would...*
   - *If I had all the time in the world, I would...*

2. Recall an idea you've entertained for a long time — maybe since you were a kid.

3. For the next week, pay attention to your thoughts. Jot down ideas that come back to you over and over.

## HELPFUL HINT:

*If you're having trouble discovering your compelling idea, or if you simply want to dream more, consider the following:*

1. **Find a place to dream.** Where do you go to dream? Is there a special place or activity that allows your mind to roam free? If you aren't sure, ask yourself:
   - *Is there a place that makes my heart beat faster?*
   - *Is there a place that I can't explain to other people?*
   - *Where do I feel most comfortable?*
   - *Where do I feel challenged?*
   - *Where do I go to be alone?*

2. **Let yourself daydream.** Get comfortable, let your mind wander, and see where your thoughts take you.
   - *Turn off the TV. Music is fine and may even help.*
   - *Be a kid again.*
   - *Don't think about work or what you're going to cook for dinner.*
   - *Keep logical thoughts out of your mind.*
   - *Don't censor; no idea is too crazy, too big, or too daunting.*

## TIPS:

*Schedule time to dream.*
*Visit your place to dream often.*

*I dream my painting, then I paint my dream.*

VINCENT VAN GOGH

# 2

# INSPIRING WORDS
## Write Down Your Dream

*Writing a dream in vivid detail, as a powerful and heartfelt story, provides the inspiration you need to make your dream come true. You will read and reread your words often. With the excitement they generate, you'll never wonder why you're in that ocean, building that house, or writing at midnight. You'll always know what you're accomplishing.*

~

For three months after my holiday trip home, the idea of swimming the Mississippi seeped into my life. It followed me everywhere until, unable to ignore it any longer, I made a decision. On a sun-soaked Friday in March, after an early morning delivery, I hurried back to the office.

In a cramped cubicle, sitting at an IKEA desk I had assembled two days earlier, I turned on the computer. Like an old-fashioned reporter in a late-night movie, my fingers flew over the keyboard trying to keep pace with the whirlwind in my head.

With each click of a key, my smile grew larger. "I'll start my swim in the summer of 1997 in Minneapolis…I'll finish by fall…There will be donors to support my cause…The media will jump on board...Millions will hear about my journey and MS...Money for research will pour in..."

Years of swimming competitions had fueled my addiction to adrenaline. I would stand on the starting block at a Big East Swim Championship and feel its rush. It would propel me to the other side of the pool and back faster than I thought possible. Now, adrenaline and I typed sixty words a minute.

I wrote about diving into the swift currents of a powerful river, feeling the water's warmth against my body, and seeing the choppy waves splashing against the shore. I would start in the city where my parents grew up, stopping each night in tiny towns with one stoplight on Main Street and a diner where I would eat greasy hamburgers and meet the locals.

I wrote about my dad and his enormous grin, and described him walking with a bounce in his step, MS no longer a part of his life.

Finally, the scene I had sketched a thousand times in my mind — that last day coming ashore: "I'm stepping onto dry land in the blaze of the Louisiana sun. The riverbank is lined with friends and supporters and I hear shouts. 'Nick, you did it! You did it!' Reporters and cameras surround me. My eyes search the shore until I spot my mom, dad, and brothers. I grab my dad and hug him. He's crying. My mom is crying. Everyone is cheering. We pop open a large bottle of champagne, pour glasses for everyone and toast to each other, to swimming a long river, to a cure for MS. I can't stop smiling."

An hour later, I leaned back in my chair, exhausted. I printed my dream.

Like Kevin Costner in *Field of Dreams* when he heard the voice that said, "If you build it, he will come," I had no idea how I would accomplish what I had just written. It didn't matter. There are times when you have to say, "What the hell? What do I have to lose? And look at what I have to gain."

# LESSON #2
## *Write down your dream*

Writing down your dream helps it come alive. The inspiring words you've written generate excitement. They'll start you on your journey and give you a boost whenever you encounter a roadblock.

Write your story in the present tense. Make it heartfelt and moving. Don't worry about sounding cocky or grandiose. Don't think about what you have to do to make it happen.

Once you've written your dream, you'll want to share it with those you trust and, later, with the world. Then rejoice — you're on your way to shouting, "I did it!"

**Focus on the big picture.** *When you're dreaming, nothing is too wild or impossible. Write your dream, resisting the temptation to get mired in details. Thinking about finances or time commitments too early may bring your dream to a screeching halt. You will need to bring your intellectual skills in later, but, for now, imagine blue skies and eagles.*

Every time I read my description of coming on shore the last day of my journey, I was filled with anticipation. Imagine if I had written about the endless minutiae of the project instead; if I had focused on:

- My training — over five hundred hours
- Getting immunizations: yellow fever, typhoid fever, hepatitis A and B, tetanus
- Losing fifteen pounds before the swim
- Finding the perfect name for the project
- Designing a logo, stationery, envelopes
- Developing brochures and fundraising flyers
- Opening a bank account and renting a P.O. box
- Finding the perfect 1-800 number
- Plotting a route
- Making calls, calls, calls. Leaving messages. More calls, calls, calls
- Financing the project
- Obtaining donated supplies:
    Inflatable dinghy…motor for the dinghy…escort boat…swim suits and goggles…sun-tan lotion (gallons)…wetsuits…video camera…35mm camera…film…printing…cell phone…Powerbars…gallons of Gatorade…lifejackets…
- Finding donated hotels, motels, or houses
- Recruiting help
- Searching for boat drivers
- Developing a fundraising plan
- Contacting media across the country

Writing press releases
Organizing press conferences
Building, updating, and promoting a Web site
Designing and selling T-shirts
ETC., ETC., ETC.

WHEW — this list still makes me cringe. If I had written my dream focusing on even a few of the hundreds of details or decisions I would face, my dream would now be crumpled in a ball, rotting in a California landfill.

**Tell those you trust.** *Until you share your dream with others, it won't feel real. Find those exceptional people capable of looking at your idea through rose-colored glasses, and then let them in on your dream and excitement. But remember, even if they don't share your enthusiasm, it's* **your** *dream. You're the one who will make it happen.*

I called my finished product a *treatment*, a term borrowed from television production that had been a part of my work life. Somehow, *treatment* sounded more impressive than *idea*. Over the next few weeks, I polished it until it told my story perfectly.

Finally, the time seemed right to share it with my parents. I called to make airline reservations for a summer trip home. In the meantime, I couldn't resist teasing my mom, who always wants to know everything about her kids.

"Mom, I have a surprise for you."

"How exciting. What is it?" she asked.

"It's a surprise."

"Come on," she pleaded.

"Okay, one hint. It's an outline for a project that I'm planning for the future."

Now she was really dying to know what it was. She fired more questions at me, hoping I'd slip. No chance. I had to do this in person, when I could watch my parents' faces. They've never been good at concealing their thoughts. I wanted to see for myself what they truly thought of the idea.

I flew to Maryland. My ten-minute wait in line to deplane consumed the little patience I had. Barely in my parents' front door, I ended my mom's (and my) tortured suspense and handed her the treatment. She scrounged through her purse for her reading glasses and then left the room to read the three pages that would change our lives.

I heard, "Whoa…Whoa…Whoa…" loud, soft, in high and low pitches, as she walked back into the den. She handed it to my dad then questioned me quietly, without giving away the contents of the document.

"Can you do it?" she asked.

"YES," fell out of my mouth.

Why did I answer yes? What did I know about swimming any river, let alone the Mississippi? I had never even seen the Mississippi River from closer than 30,000 feet. It didn't matter. I had made up my mind to do it, and nothing was going to stop me.

My dad finished reading, wiped his eyes, and let out a long sigh. What was he thinking? Was he happy, worried, upset, or what? This time I couldn't tell.

"What can we do to help?" he asked. At that moment, I knew my Swim would happen.

A few days later, we met John and Andy in Cape May, New Jersey, for a family weekend at the beach and my chance to share my plans with them. Instead of telling me my idea was crazy, they responded with the same enthusiasm as my parents.

"When are you planning to swim?" was John's first question.

"Within two years," I replied.

They could have asked me the next logical question, "*How* are you going to do it?" I'm sure they knew I didn't have an answer, so neither asked. Both offered their help. Amazing.

***Tell the world.*** *When you announce your dream to the world, you gain more incentive to make it happen. Tell your coworkers, boss, and the person next to you at the gym. Tell your story to the cab driver taking you to the airport. Break the silence in the elevator by sharing it with your fellow riders. Announce it to anyone and everyone. Put the pressure on to make it happen.*

Two days before the start of my Swim, at 6:30 in the morning, I stood next to my dad on a steep bank overlooking the Mississippi River and watched my breath. On this unseasonably cool Friday, a morning fog cast a chilly haze over the Minneapolis skyline in the background.

We were wired with microphones. I was having a hard time getting the coiled earpiece to stay in my ear. Every time I smiled, it would fall out and I couldn't stop smiling. My dad, forever his kids' cheerleader, beamed. He loved being a part of it all.

Until that day, my dad had only told a few people about his MS. He was afraid of the reaction he might receive from his patients and colleagues. They might not understand that MS affected his ability to walk, not his ability to be a good doctor. If anyone asked about his limp, he would pull out any one of his stories: "I have a bad back," or "...a sore hip," or "...(fill in the blank for the day's coverup)." He now had the courage to announce his MS on national TV. I felt proud standing next to him.

While we waited to talk with Joan Lunden on *Good Morning America*, we made small talk with the producers of the show (whom I pictured sitting in a warm control booth in New York City). I was stopped mid-sentence by a new voice, "Hello, Nick and Dr. Irons. We are about three minutes away from you. Joan Lunden isn't with us today, so Elizabeth Vargas will interview you. We'll be with you in a few minutes."

As the clock ticked down, we stood in silence. I reviewed in my mind the messages I wanted to get across: money for MS research;

350,000 people in the U.S. living with the disease; six hours of swimming, five days a week for four months; awareness; P.O. box number. My dad, unfazed by all the attention, and less than stellar at remembering names, prepared in his own unique way, writing "Elizabeth" in big bubble letters in the mud with his cane. We laughed.

I heard crackling in my earpiece, Elizabeth and Charlie Gibson chitchatting, and then the tease: "And coming up after the break, we will meet a man who is planning to swim the Mississippi River to help fight his father's illness."

After the commercial break ended, they played video shot earlier in the week explaining the Swim. Sixty seconds later, we were talking with Elizabeth. I tried to remember what to say. I think my dad used the word "Elizabeth" no fewer than three times. As quickly as it began, the interview was over.

How surreal. I had just announced to 4.5 million people on national television that I would swim the Mississippi River. Elizabeth told everyone that *Good Morning America* would check in with me along the way. The viewers now expected to follow my journey to the end. The pressure was on. I didn't want to be on TV in three weeks telling everyone why I quit. The title "First person in seventy years to *attempt* to swim the Mississippi River" was not in my picture.

## MAKE IT HAPPEN

LESSON #2: *Write down your dream.*

You now have your compelling idea. Complete the following activity to transform this idea into a dream.

1. Tell your story on paper. The following advice will help you bring your dream to life.
   - *Write in the present tense.*
   - *Make it heartfelt.*
   - *Concentrate on the exact moment your dream is coming true.*
   - *Describe that moment in the first person.*
     *Who is surrounding you?*
     *What do you see, hear, or taste?*
     *How do you feel?*
   - *Turn off that part of your brain that asks, "How can I do this?"*
   - *Capture the excitement.*

   Now you have a dream to share with others.

2. Tell a family member, a close friend, or a co-worker. Show them the excitement you are feeling.

3. Once you have the support of those close to you, announce it to the world. Share your story with a larger group. Tell your soccer team, church group, book club, or post it on your Web site. Put the pressure on to make it happen.

*A strong passion…will insure success,
for the desire of the end will point out the means.*

WILLIAM HAZLITT

# 3

# A ROADMAP YOU WON'T HAVE TO FOLD
## Make a Plan

*A master plan, filled with the details of your journey, will guide you toward your destination. Whether it's scribbled on a napkin, laid out in great detail on a spreadsheet, or stored in the compartments of your mind, a plan gives you direction. You'll always know where you're going and how to get there.*

~

My brothers and I traveled a lot with our parents when we were kids. These trips are the source of some of my family's favorite stories. No one lets my mom forget the extra cab-load of fifteen suitcases we toted to Italy when we brought my grandfather back to visit his homeland. We recount in vivid detail the frightening night on China Airlines when we circled the Shanghai airport for an hour, the plane flailing, bolts of lightning lighting up the sky, and strains of "Amazing Grace", sung by a group of terrified American tourists, filling the air inside. Like the journeys of my childhood, our family embarked on a new adventure.

"We need a plan."

John's words made me dizzy. My stomach churned. My palms sweat. Like many dreamers, I suffer from "plan-o-phobia." The mere sound of his words sent terror through my body and created a sudden urge to flee.

I knew that when we designed a plan I would have to answer probing questions. "How much will it cost? Where will we find support boats, supplies, hotels? Is it safe? Is it legal to swim in the Mississippi?"

"Okay," I reluctantly agreed.

During our planning sessions, everyone found a role. John loves an intellectual challenge. A Ph.D. candidate at MIT and the resident genius in our family, he focused our efforts on bringing order to the mind-numbing logistics of the Swim — asking all those questions I knew I would finally have to answer, starting with finding an attention-grabbing name for the project. For once, I appreciated his intelligence, which has always given him the advantage when playing monopoly, chess, or poker.

Andy, the actor and playwright, spiced our plan conversations with passion. As the project evolved, he asked *why* as well as *how*. In the midst of never-ending details, he reminded us of our motivation for making the Swim a success, encouraging us to keep in mind the ultimate prize, an end for multiple sclerosis.

He also played the role of mediator. With skills honed as the youngest trying to resolve the inevitable battles that occur among brothers, he calmed us when we yelled our opposing ideas at each other. He often resorted to comedy, drama, or song and dance — whatever it took for us to see the humor of arguing over which company to contact for goggles.

My mom was my Prozac. I lived with the gnawing feeling that at any time a major problem could drown the Swim. From figuring out a way to get our supplies to Minneapolis to finding someone to donate a logo design, she was my constant reassurance that nothing would stop my dream.

My dad loved picking up the minute details tossed aside by the rest of us. The smaller the detail, the more he relished it. He was always there to dot the i's and cross the t's — literally — proofreading every piece of correspondence or marketing material we wrote. I'm convinced he never met a comma he didn't like.

I needed and appreciated my family. Working together, we were powerful. We did it for our dad; we did it for each other. Each of us was invaluable. Without the contribution of even one, the Swim may not have happened.

These initial discussions took place at my parents' home in Maryland during Christmas break, 1995. We then went our separate ways — John to Boston, Andy to Saratoga Springs, and me to L.A.

In January 1996, John, in the midst of his doctorate, began putting together the Web site. At the time, personal Web sites were rare, but John realized the potential of using the Internet to increase exposure to the Swim and spread information about MS. He spent months designing a state-of-the-art site that included a page for our digital pictures and a daily report from the River. After the Swim began, he updated the site each day from his home in Boston. Even if supporters lived hundreds of miles away, they could travel with us.

Andy went back to finish his senior year at Skidmore before joining me at the start of the Swim in Minneapolis. My dad returned to his busy allergy practice and his sneezing and wheezing patients (all of whom continued to be patients even after he announced his MS on national TV); they loved sharing his newfound celebrity.

My mom and I, with a sketchy outline in hand, spent hours on the phone pulling all the pieces together. With no experience in fundraising, public relations, or marketing, our preparation for the Swim was a year and a half of trial and error. We pursued whatever seemed logical. We followed only one rule: when in doubt, pick up the phone. Someone will always help if you make enough calls to find the right person.

In the fall of 1996, we were ready to look for sponsors to finance the Swim through cash or donated supplies. I assumed responsibility for bringing corporations on board. Nike seemed like a logical first try. From my living room couch in Los Angeles, I called Nike's corporate offices in Beaverton, Oregon.

"Good morning," I said in my most professional voice. "I'm planning a major fundraising event for multiple sclerosis, and I'm in the process of looking for corporate sponsors. Could you please tell me who I need to speak with?"

After a series of transfers, I was telling my story for the fourth time. Success — I had the name of the marketing executive to contact.

With a computer but no printer, and no extra money to buy one, I worked out a system with my parents. I found the names of executives at large companies like Coca-Cola, Gatorade, and Farmers Insurance, then went to Kinko's and faxed the list of information to my parents. Each weekend for six months, they personalized sponsorship letters using these names and addresses. They printed the letters, stuffed, licked, and stamped the envelopes, and drove to the post office to mail the requests. I followed up a week later with a phone call, or more likely, with two, three, or however many necessary to convince the right person to help.

Nike decided to take a chance on us and sent a package filled with all the goggles, swimsuits, and towels we needed or could ever want. A small start, but a start nonetheless. With the Nike name behind us, we began adding sponsors.

By January 1997, plans for the Swim started falling into place. I began to breathe easier as we crossed off important items on our multiple lists. Nearly a dozen sponsors were lined up. Everything from sun-tan lotion to an Avon inflatable boat had been promised. My dad planned the mileage of the day-to-day schedule. I was training. Only one major hole — a large black hole, like the ones you see on PBS — loomed out there, threatening to swallow everything in sight.

My mom started ending every conversation with, "Nick, we need to put a big push on getting a boat."

She was referring to an escort boat, a craft large enough to protect me from barges, pleasure boats, and Jet Skiers. It would be a place for shelter from storms and a refuge for refueling and rehydrating breaks. Because safety for everyone involved was a prime consideration, the Swim wasn't going to happen without a boat.

We called anyone and everyone we could think of — marinas, boat manufacturers, yachting clubs — but no one was jumping on board. My parents began canvassing boat shows on weekends.

What was the big deal? We were just asking to borrow a $100,000 boat to use for four months on a dangerous river.

January — no boat.

February — no boat.

March — no boat.

April — no boat.

May 7 — *Good Morning America* joined the boat-less adventure. We had 4.5 million people ready to follow me down the Mississippi River that I was determined to swim. Three weeks before kickoff — no boat. The black hole sucked a little harder.

Even if we found a boat, we had no drivers. My mom decided to try a new approach. At the National Capital Boat Show, she learned about the United States Power Squadrons, the largest boating-enthusiast group in the country with more than 60,000 members. She called Lance Jensen, rear commander of marketing for the Power Squadrons. Surely, they would have someone who would be willing to pilot a boat for us...assuming we got one.

After months of worry, within one day, Lance not only promised us a tag-team escort of Power Squadrons members, but also boats. The ingenious plan: Power Squadrons member #1 would take his or her boat, meet up with us at a designated marina and travel with us for a set period of time. Power Squadrons member #2 would then join us for the next leg of the journey. This escort switch was to happen, like clockwork, every day or two. It sounded complicated, but it could work.

Lance, our guardian angel, fell out of the sky to plug our black hole. Thanks to his creativity and kind-heartedness and the generosity of individual members, The United States Power Squadrons became an integral part of the success of the *Mississippi Swim for Multiple Sclerosis* (MS4MS). Our escorts became our companions and protectors.

By kickoff on June 1, we had our plan in place. After eighteen months of organizing, training, and fundraising, I was convinced that the hard part was over. Nothing could possibly be any more difficult than the previous year and a half. Only a 1,550-mile, four-month swim down an unknown river remained.

# LESSON #3
## Make a Plan

A well-thought-out plan will be your roadmap to your destination. Putting a plan on paper in great detail will help you think through and keep up with the numerous details you'll face. With a plan, you can set intermediate goals — stepping-stones to your dream. Will you need a team of volunteers? If so, how many? Who will they be? When do you need them?

A written plan can be created in many different formats. If you're detail-oriented, a formal spreadsheet may soothe your need for order. If you're artistic, you may want a sketch of each area of the whole project. Prepare a master plan that fits your personality and feels right to you. Then, set priorities and develop a timeline to complete the necessary tasks.

With your plan always close at hand, you'll know what you have to do and when you have to do it — the keys to accomplishing your dream.

**Choose a planning style that fits you.** *There is no "correct" way to devise a plan. Some people like simple outlines; others find spreadsheets work best. You might want to brainstorm alone or with a group. Choose a method that feels right to you.*

When we started planning the Swim, my mom used the "list" method. She had pages of yellow, legal-sized, lined paper filled with lists — lists of overall goals, lists of supplies, lists of potential sponsors, lists of media. She will never admit it, but I know she had lists of the lists we needed to make.

My plan-o-phobia roared out of control.

Soon it became obvious that we needed a more organized plan. My parents gathered five of their friends together to "Storyboard," a method of brainstorming that my mom had learned years before. Back in L.A., I attended by phone. With overwhelming logistics and multiple goals for the Swim, it proved to be a more efficient method of planning than the lists. In several two-hour sessions, we created a giant outline of the project, using brightly colored index cards, magic markers, and a corkboard.

With a little wine and a lot of creativity, the group divided the project into major categories (headings). These included logistics, fundraising, finances, volunteers, PR, media, and supplies.

From there, each of these *headings* was broken into *subheadings*. "Supplies," for example, had several subheadings: food, boat needs, safety needs, etc. Each of these was broken into even smaller pieces — "safety needs" had many *sub-subheadings*: sun-tan lotion, wetsuits, first-aid kit, lifejackets, and a radio to name a few.

After completing the outline, we displayed the brightly colored index cards on a corkboard in my parents' office. Headings, subheadings, and sub-subheadings helped everyone keep track of the intermediate goals and details of the project.

Over the next few months the storyboard was modified again and again. It served well as a general plan that gave some semblance of sanity to what was, in fact, a logistical nightmare.

**Set priorities.** *Every plan will be filled with endless tasks, some more urgent than others. Decide what must be done and then set priorities. Tackle each one in order of importance, so you can avoid wasting energy.*

During our first family planning session, it became obvious that we needed one vital piece of information before we could go further. I didn't have the heart to pursue the question that had the potential of dashing my dream, so my mom volunteered for the job. It became top priority. She called the U.S. Army Corps of Engineers, the agency responsible for overseeing the Mississippi, and posed the critical question to officials in several states along the River: "Is it legal to swim in the Mississippi?"

She heard varying responses:

"I don't know."

"Let me call you back."

"Nobody has ever asked me that before."

Without definitive *no's*, we assumed that they all meant: It may not be legal, but it's not illegal; don't worry about getting official permission.

I sighed a giddy sigh. That was easy. Scratch the first concern off the list. I would not break any laws or be thrown into jail for this adventure. On to the next priority…and the next…and the next.

**Develop a timeline.** *Time considerations are crucial in planning any dream. Use a timeline to set a date to complete your dream. Then, use it to create a schedule for finishing each task. Some items can be completed with a phone call in a matter of minutes. Others may take weeks or months. Plot each on a timeline, keeping in mind your priorities. You'll stay on top of the important tasks and deadlines necessary to make your dream happen.*

I knew my swim would be difficult. While others worried about the pollution, barges, and debris, in my mind only two obstacles stood between me and success.

First, I was a sprinter. For years as a competitive swimmer, my forte had always been the 50- or 100-yard breaststroke — or any stroke for a distance of less than a minute. I could be competitive with anyone for one length of the pool, fast for two, slower for four, and miserable beyond that. A 1,550-mile swim meant a transformation from sprinter to distance swimmer.

Second, I was a breaststroker, excelling in the slowest and least efficient of the four strokes in competitive swimming. Breaststroke would never get me down the Mississippi River, or, if it did, not very fast. I had to change my stroke.

With only eighteen months to accomplish these two objectives, a schedule for workouts and a timeline to complete my training was crucial. I began in earnest to be ready by June 1997.

I dove into a pool in early 1996, after a two-year swimming hiatus, to begin a year and a half of training. Living in L.A. gave me access to Southern California Aquatics (SCAQ), a large Master's swim team. The team was founded and coached by Clay Evans and Bonnie Adair, who had consistently produced national and world champions. I needed their expertise to guide me and push me to my limits.

I devised a timeline for my training schedule. I started slowly, swimming an hour a day three days a week for the first three months. After acclimating my body to that shock, I increased my workouts to an hour a day, five days a week — another three months. Then two and three hours per day until I was comfortably swimming four hours a day, five days a week.

Weekends during my last six months of training offered me an opportunity to up my workouts and add a bit of variety to my swim schedule. On Saturday mornings, I joined seventy-five other Masters swimmers at the Santa Monica College pool. By 8:30 we would have completed a short warm-up, followed by a thirty-minute main set — four 500s (twenty lengths of the pool followed by ten seconds of rest). Kicking, pulling, and sprinting drills rounded out the practice.

By 10:30, I would meet a friend in Manhattan Beach and walk two miles to the Hermosa Beach Pier. We pulled on wetsuits and waded into the fifty-three degree water of the Pacific Ocean. We swam for a couple of hours and I stayed for a bit of body surfing afterward.

Two hours later, I'd be back at Santa Monica College to change into my still-wet swimsuit for another practice. I jumped in the water starting right where I left off. More 500s. More kicking. More pulling. More sprinting.

Putting my social life on hold (at least for a night), I crawled into bed before nine o'clock. Less than twelve hours later, I made my way back to the Santa Monica College pool.

In addition, I spent hours in Borders Books reading *Total Immersion*, *Swimming Even Faster*, and *Swimming into the 21st Century*, learning the fine points of swim technique. My natural instinct had always been to muscle my way to the other end of the pool, like I muscle my way through everything in life. I was kicking too hard and my pull was slow and inefficient. I knew I couldn't use that technique on my way down the Mississippi River. It's just too exhausting. By paying attention to my stroke, noticing how my hands moved through the water, I discovered how I could get more out of each movement.

As I began to muscle less, I was no longer plowing through the water like a Mack truck. Instead, I concentrated on slicing through, like a Ferrari or Lamborghini. I became obsessed with taking the fewest strokes possible across a twenty-five yard pool. I began counting my strokes: One-two-three-four-five-six-seven-eight-nine-ten-flip. One-two-three-four-five-six-seven-eight-nine-ten-flip. Over and over and over again.

After swimming for a year and a half on this schedule, I gained strength, technique, and confidence, and overcame my two biggest obstacles. Now, as a distance freestyler, I was ready to challenge a long, long river.

## MAKE IT HAPPEN

### LESSON #3: *Make a plan*

Now that you have a dream that excites you, prepare a plan. The following activities will help you in the process.

### TIP:

*Using colored index cards and magic markers will make these activities easier. Use one card for each idea.*

1. Start by writing a two- or three-word title for your dream.

2. Write down, on separate cards, three or four of your most important objectives. What do you want to accomplish by making your dream come true?

3. Ask yourself, "What do I have to think about or do to make my dream come true?" Take fifteen minutes to brainstorm. Write down everything that comes to mind.
Remember:
   - *Have fun.*
   - *Be creative.*
   - *Don't censor your thoughts.*
   - *Write as fast as you can.*
   - *There is no "right" answer.*
   - *Don't worry about how you will complete each task.*

4. Sort through the ideas you just wrote. Keep those that make sense to you. Find the nuggets of wisdom in the creative ideas you discovered. Throw out any that don't fit all the objectives of your dream. (For example: giving away MS4MS T-shirts may have been a fine goodwill idea, but it would not have fit our objective of raising money for MS research.)

5. Organize ideas that relate to each other by placing them into groups. (For example, our ideas were divided into categories such as: PR, Fundraising, Logistics, and Volunteers.)

6. Once your ideas are organized, make an outline.

7. Prioritize. Go through your outline and label each task as:
    - *Totally Necessary*
    - *Important, but not Crucial*
    - *Nice to Have*

8. Develop time criteria. Begin with the tasks in the "Totally Necessary" category. Attach start and completion dates to each item. Continue with the other two categories.
   Remember:
    - *Many tasks will overlap on your timeline, but you can do multiple tasks at once.*

9. Display your timeline.
   Suggestions:
    - *Post a huge calendar on your wall.*
    - *Draw a horizontal timeline with day, week, or month intervals.*
    - *Use different colored markers to distinguish between priority categories.*
    - *Design a Microsoft Excel spreadsheet.*

> *Happiness isn't good enough for me!
> I demand euphoria!*
>
> CALVIN (BILL WATTERSON)

# 4

# THE TIME OF YOUR LIFE
## Have Fun

*Although many dreams have "serious" outcomes, to succeed
in completing your goal you have to like what you're doing,
have fun, and laugh a lot. Having fun helps you swim a long river,
explore the deepest cave, or gaze through a microscope for hours
on end. Laughter keeps you sane and happy along the way
to making your dream come true.*

~

By eleven o'clock on Sunday, June 1, 1997, a crowd had appeared on an oak- and elm-lined bank overlooking the Mississippi River in Minneapolis. Gathered were my grandparents, aunt, uncle and cousins, good friends from my parents' past, strangers who'd read the morning article announcing the Swim in the *Minneapolis Star Tribune* or *St. Paul Pioneer Press*, and the media including a local news helicopter circling over-head. Green-and-white *Mississippi Swim for Multiple Sclerosis* T-shirts and a buzz of excitement surrounded me.

I was about to plunge into the muddy water of the Mississippi and begin the journey that had consumed my life for more than eighteen months. My finish line…four months away.

From the moment Andy and I landed in Minneapolis a week prior to kickoff, frigid rain became our constant companion. Either a drenching downpour or an ever-present mist accompanied us as we traipsed around the Twin Cities finishing our never-ending errands.

The wet weather chilled us as we hunted for the out-of-the-way boating-supply superstore where we picked up extra lifejackets. It numbed our hands as we inflated an eleven-foot dinghy, which would become Andy's "home" for the next four months.

The mist fell on our shoulders as we hiked down a slippery, steep bank to the water's edge to scope out a possible kickoff site for our departure. In that cold drizzle at the River's edge, on the evening before we left, Andy learned the basics of boating from a willing Power Squadrons member — how to tie a bowline knot, the difference between bow and stern, and how to start a stubborn motor. It was a crash course in nautical safety for someone whose boating experience was limited to piloting a red jet boat — his favorite bathtub toy when he was five.

Where were the fluffy white clouds and eagles flying overhead and seventy-five degree weather I had imagined for the last eighteen months?

Happily, on Sunday, the day of departure, blue skies had pushed out dreary black clouds and the temperature neared the mid-seventies. The sun warmed the air, but did little for the fifty-six-degree River.

Before I could begin, I had to change into my wetsuit. The only convenient place to do this was a port-o-potty on the bank of the River. Squeezed into the cramped space, standing on my tennis shoes, I attempted, in Houdini-like fashion, to change into my skintight protective suit without touching the walls, floor, or anything else in this rank structure.

I stepped out of the makeshift dressing room to face the rapid-fire clicks and whizzes of camera shutters. Crews from the Associated Press, *Good Morning America*, four TV stations, and two newspapers, less than an arm's length away, aimed their lenses.

This was it. This was my start. This was the moment I would remember for the rest of my life.

"Wait! Wait! Wait! Nick. Nick." A short, little man peeked out from the mass of reporters three feet in front of me.

"I'm sorry, Nick, but I wasn't ready. Could you go back in and come out again?"

"Okaaay." I turned back into the all-too-familiar space.

"Ready?" I yelled.

I heard the same voice, "Could you count down from three, so we'll know *exactly* when you're coming out?"

I flashed back to my childhood...playing hide-and-seek... standing in a corner of our den counting before running off to find my brothers who had found some new hiding place. "Three, two, one. Here I come."

*This* was it. *This* was my start. *This* was the moment that I would remember for the rest of my life.

Throwing open the green plastic door, with a touch of drama that I borrowed from watching Andy perform onstage, I made another appearance and headed toward my family standing at the water's edge. The throng of reporters in front of me gingerly walked backward down the steep hill, precariously balancing cumbersome video cameras on their shoulders.

I sped up. They tried to keep their distance. I slowed down, quickly stopped, and watched as momentum kept them going backward...further and further. Would they stop before they fell into the River? Were they having as much fun as I was?

Halfway to the water's edge, I stopped to pull my wetsuit onto my arms and chest. The clicks of the shutters increased to a frenetic pace. Somehow, adjusting my wetsuit seemed like a historic moment to the camera people. How bizarre.

I hugged my mom first, grateful for all the work she had done to make this moment possible. Then I headed toward my dad.

We hugged. As I pulled away, I noticed a single tear running down his cheek.

I waded into the icy waters, raised my arms overhead, and lunged forward. Pulling one arm over the other, my dream was no longer 30,000 feet in the air, but fully immersed in the Great River. Like a swarm of bees, the well-wishers followed me, running along the rocky shoreline by my side, clapping and cheering.

"Go, Nick!"

I stroked ahead.

"Good luck, Nick!"

My heart pounded.

Through the waves, I searched for my dad each time I took a breath. Off to my left, I spotted him standing statue-like, stuck in one spot on the shore. He couldn't command his legs to run with everyone else. Gripping his dog-headed cane in his right hand, he waved broad arches with his left. His face looked like a billboard with "I Love You" painted in bold letters. I watched as he became smaller and smaller, alone on the riverbank.

"Have fun!" I heard him yell as I dipped my head back into the muddy water.

# LESSON #4
## *Have Fun*

To succeed in completing any goal, you have to like what you're doing, have fun, and laugh a lot. If you're not enjoying yourself, all the frustrating moments or monotonous tasks that are a part of any dream will tempt you to run for the nearest exit.

When you're having fun, your creativity soars and solutions to problems are at your fingertips. You'll find a way to swim a long river or reach the peak of the highest mountain. Leave fun behind and your dream will languish on the shore.

Humor is everywhere. Look for it in your world and laugh at yourself. Use it and enjoy its power.

**Use laughter to keep you sane.** *Laughing hard and often lifts the burdens of any endeavor. It's easy to get embroiled in details or day-to-day annoyances while pursuing your dream. Laugh and big issues won't seem so big. Monotony won't seem so monotonous. Laughing will give you the perspective needed to keep you sane.*

The Mississippi River is often dubbed the Big Muddy. It didn't take long for me to understand why. Swimming in its murky water was not only a daunting physical challenge, but an enormous mental one as well.

Imagine pulling arm over arm, swimming in a steady rhythm, for five hours every day. Now, imagine that you can't see your arms in front of you or anything in the water below you — not even the fish (which is not necessarily a bad thing). The murky waters of the river impair your vision. You are virtually blind.

You have less than a second to glimpse to the side while you take a breath every other stroke. Vast muddy water and an occasional glance at your guide in a small boat ahead of you is the limit of your view until you reach your five-minute break thirty minutes later. Now imagine your head is underwater ninety percent of the time, so you can't hear much except the sound of splashing as your arms enter the water. The only people in your life are fifteen feet ahead and fifty feet behind. It's you and the blurred river for four months.

It didn't take long for the excitement of the kickoff to fade into the reality of endless lonely hours of repetition. Sheer boredom overwhelmed me.

I was shocked. For the most part I had trained in swimming pools where I at least had something to look at — lines on the bottom. In some pools, you can count tiles. Sometimes, you can look at other people, even say a couple of words between laps. I know these things don't sound like a lot to non-swimmers, but believe me they make a difference.

As you can probably imagine, I had to find something to keep my mind occupied. I tried counting my strokes — 1,006, 1,007, 1,008…a surefire road to insanity.

I tried reciting the grammar I'd learned during my seven years of German class in middle school, high school, and college, but that lasted about seven minutes before I drew a blank. How many times could I repeat the sentence, "The big black dog is tired." *"Der große schwarze Hund ist Müde."*

And then one day, quite by accident, I started replaying Seinfeld episodes in my head. I astounded myself with how many lines, scenes, and characters I remembered. Totally amused, I thought about George Costanza fighting with "The Bubble Boy" over the correct Trivial Pursuit answer: Moops vs. Moors. I heard George yelling, "It's *Moops*." And the Bubble Boy screaming, "*Moors*, you idiot!" The next scene — George being chased by irate townspeople after he accidentally punctures the boy's protective bubble — kept me swimming another mile.

I chuckled at Jerry in a bakery musing on world peace: "Look to the cookie, Elaine. Look to the cookie." Jerry's theory was that racial harmony could be achieved if we just studied the black-and-white cookie.

I laughed, sometimes inhaling a gulp of the gooey stuff I was swimming in. After this breakthrough, the once-dreaded swimming sets went a lot faster. I was laughing, having fun, and crossing off the miles.

**Use fun to solve a problem.** *When you're laughing, you're less likely to get caught up in "I can't." Ease your stress by having fun and, like magic, everything will seem possible. When you're enjoying yourself, you can uncover a solution to any problem and find creative ways to make your dream happen.*

Andy and I had an amazing ability to get along. Together all day, every day for four months, with all the annoyances of the trip —

heat, bugs, exhaustion — we always laughed. When times were tough, we laughed even harder and conjured up a creative solution to any problem.

At the end of each day, we found ourselves in another city or town, staying in another motel or hotel. One night, we checked into a six-room motel on the outskirts of a town of 2,000. It wasn't exactly The Ritz-Carlton. Let's face it — it wasn't exactly the Holiday Inn.

On this late afternoon, I enjoyed a hot shower and was vigorously scrubbing the Mississippi River off my body when I heard a crack of thunder and noticed raindrops on the bathroom window. With a head full of shampoo, I watched the lights flicker.

"Oh no. Please no."

Lounging on a bed, no matter how lumpy, flipping through the three available channels, and eating a pepperoni pizza seemed like heaven that evening. I climbed out of the shower, grabbed a threadbare towel and the lights went off — for good. We were stuck in the middle of nowhere, without power.

I threw on some jeans and walked into the bedroom. "Andy, we have to get out of here. Let's go somewhere. Anywhere."

The thought of sitting around a dark motel room all night was getting scarier by the minute.

"Did you forget? We don't have a car," Andy reminded me.

Like the city boy that I am, I headed to the nightstand, pulled out the dog-eared, twenty-page phone book, and looked up the word "Taxi."

I mumbled to myself while flipping through the well-worn pages. "Let's see, taxi, taxi…tax preparation, taxidermy…no taxi. Okay…maybe it's under 'Cab.' No cab listings, either."

Running out of ideas, we left our powerless room and walked to the road. I looked at Andy and said, "You know, we could walk the three miles to Pizza Hut."

Who was I kidding? We both knew that wasn't going to

happen. I engaged in no physical activity after I finished my twelve-mile swim, and Andy engaged in no physical activity, period.

At least the rain had stopped. I thrust my thumb into the air. After a few minutes, Andy joined in, reasoning that two thumbs were better than one. We looked at each other and howled.

My parents taught us growing up that everyone who hitchhikes in this country is at one time or another chopped into small pieces and stored in someone's basement. I have always equated hitchhiking with a gruesome, horrible death. But that day, it held the tempting prospect of pizza, Coke, and lights.

Car after car, truck after truck, passed without stopping. We didn't look that bad, did we? Some people honked their horns and waved; others just shook their heads and laughed. We had never hitchhiked, so I reasoned that maybe we didn't have the right attitude, or the right look. Maybe we were just too male. No one wanted to pick up two men hitchhiking.

Just as we were about to give up, Andy turned and noticed a disheveled man walking across the motel parking lot.

"Excuse me," Andy yelled. The man looked over.

"Excuse me, do you have a car?"

"Sho' do," he answered, in the thickest drawl I had ever heard.

"Would you like to give us a ride into town?" How could anyone pass up a request like that?

"Where ya wanna go?"

"Pizza Hut?"

His squinty eyes scanned our bodies from head to toe. A faint smile parted his lips exposing a few missing teeth. And then a wink.

"Well, lemme git ma truck." He sauntered out of sight, and moments later, our knight in shining armor drove up in his rusted Chevy pickup. He leaned across the tattered, once-blue upholstery of the passenger seat and swung open the creaking door. "C'mon in!"

"Andy, you get in first," I whispered.

"I'm not getting in. *You get in.*"

"Get in," I demanded.

"Nick, this was your idea. You get in."

We tried to be polite, as Andy and I (in the opposite order) climbed into the aging, gun-racked cab. I heard my parents warning us, "NEVER, EVER, UNDER ANY CIRCUMSTANCES, HITCHHIKE."

For the first few minutes we made giddy small talk. Anything to keep his mind occupied. He seemed to like us and offered to return later to drive us back to the motel. Not wanting to push our luck, we said, "No thanks."

Luckily, my parents were wrong this time. We chuckled as we walked into the Pizza Hut. The sounds of Garth Brooks blaring from the jukebox never sounded so good. Power. We spent the evening sitting in a lumpy, red-vinyl booth, eating pepperoni pizza, watching one of the three available channels. A perfect night.

**Look for humor in your world.** *Everyday life, filled with stresses and challenges, can seem overwhelming. It's easy to get caught up in the heaviness of our circumstances. We may begin to believe that the shirt the cleaners lost is irreplaceable. Yet, even in the most serious moments, laughter can bring relief and ease a difficult time. Humor is everywhere. Pay attention and you'll find it.*

When I was working for *American Gladiators*, I answered a call one afternoon from a producer. He instructed me to pick up a prop, a "pugil stick," from our storage unit. For those of you unfamiliar with gladiator paraphernalia, pugil sticks resemble giant Q-tips and are used in a contest called *Joust*. Perched on a pedestal raised twenty feet off the ground, a Gladiator and a competitor engage in a battle for "King of the Hill" using the sticks as weapons to send each other flying.

After driving across town, I crawled through the dark, musty, crowded storage space (hoping not to come across some multi-legged creature), until I discovered the sticks in a far off corner. I pulled one out and carried it to my car.

There was a problem. The bulky object was over six feet long, with a very large padded tip on both ends. I was driving a small Acura Integra. Although spatial relationships have never been my strong suit, I quickly determined that the stick was longer than the inside of my car.

I tried placing it on a diagonal from the front passenger seat to the back window. The door wouldn't close. It fit across the backseat if I let it project two feet out the side window. Too dangerous. Finally, I opened the sunroof and positioned one end in the backseat, the other end jutting three feet into the air through the top of the car. Success.

Time to deliver the giant-sized Q-tip sporting the words "American Gladiators" protruding through the roof of my car. I felt like the Oscar Mayer Weinermobile, a giant ad driving the freeways of Los Angeles. Cars slowed, the occupants strained to read the words, then laughed when they figured it out. I laughed all the way to "Hawk's" house.

**Laugh at yourself.** *Laughing at yourself can help you keep your friends as well as your perspective. Take yourself too seriously and watch your supporters flee. It's easier than you think. We all have plenty of opportunities to see humor in ourselves. Be open to laughing at your idiosyncrasies. It comes in handy, especially when you're fulfilling your big dream.*

Madison, Wisconsin, is home to *The Onion*, a satirical newspaper of pure genius. Funny, irreverent, and politically incorrect, no topic is too sacred for this weekly publication.

One recent issue caught my attention. On the front page, I noticed a picture of what looked like a very large charity run. Thousands of participants, wearing matching T-shirts, eagerly stood at the starting line, braced to begin their event.

The headline read: "6,000 RUNNERS FAIL TO DISCOVER CURE FOR BREAST CANCER."

I was immediately hooked. The article told how runner after runner in Atlanta crossed the finish line without an answer in hand. Not one of the runners was able to find "a viable cure" for cancer anywhere along that 3.1-mile route.

To add insult to injury, the article went on to explain that recently another 3,000 cyclists in Dallas had been "unable to isolate the portion of the human genome responsible for Alzheimer's disease." And 200 rowers from twenty-seven different colleges gathered in Boston for an "unsuccessful attempt to eliminate AIDS."

They might as well have added: "After a 1,550-mile perilous swim down the Mississippi, Nick Irons has yet to find the cure for multiple sclerosis."

I couldn't stop laughing. Years of my life reduced before my eyes in one humbling article. I shared it with my family. Thousands of hours of work and we could all see a kernel of truth in this satire.

## MAKE IT HAPPEN

### LESSON #4: *Have fun*

Along the way to making your dream come true, remember to have fun and laugh. Complete the following activities to remind yourself of the importance of fun and to increase laughter in your life.

1. Recount a time when you felt stressed, or on the verge of craziness, and used humor to defuse the situation.
    - *Where were you?*
    - *What was happening?*
    - *How did humor and laughter help?*

2. For one day, pretend you're a stand-up comedian who's looking for new material. Notice what's funny or quirky about your world. What do you notice that would make other people laugh?

3. Write a joke about yourself or recall an embarrassing moment in your past. What's funny about you, your life, or that moment?

4. Take at least thirty minutes to laugh this week. If you need help, try one of these.
    - *Watch a humorous movie or TV show.*
    - *Read any book by Bill Bryson (or a humorist of your choice).*
    - *Play with your kids — or a friend's kids.*
    - *Go to a comedy club.*
    - *Call a friend who makes you laugh.*

5. Think of what would keep you entertained if you were swimming for months on end.

Me at the pool

Telling the world on *Good Morning America* — my dad and me

Kickoff — Minneapolis

Into the River for the first time

My makeshift dressing room

Still having fun

Andy looking nautical

"PR Goddess" and "Webmaster"
— Mom and John

Swimming in the Mississippi

Oops!

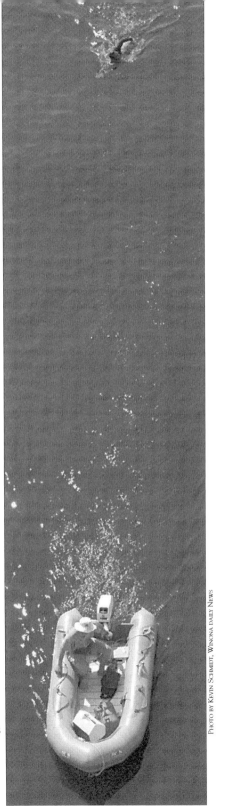

Long days

Photo by Kevin Schmidt, Winona daily News

Hanging out with Andy

Those "dam" locks

I finally meet Joe & Barbara

My dad — always the cheerleader

The Goodmans & Floyds to the rescue

*Obstacles are those frightful things you see when you take your eyes off the goal.*

HENRY FORD

# 5

# A CHANGE OF PACE
## Adjust Your Goals

*Big dreams are powerful. They give you a reason
for getting up in the morning. They can also be overwhelming.
While making your dream happen, you may begin to wonder
if you'll ever complete it. Adjusting the goals that lead to your
big dream will help you make it to the finish line.*

~

I waded into the muddy Mississippi with confidence and a plan. My dream included swimming 1,550 miles, traveling through ten states, and taking one million strokes to end on the shores of Baton Rouge.

For the first few days, propelled by adrenaline from the kickoff, I stroked twelve to fourteen miles in four or five hours. If I was stiff or sore, I never noticed. A post-card-like picture of Baton Rouge flashed into my thoughts as I counted off the miles:

Day One: 1,550 miles. Ten states. 1 million strokes. Baton Rouge.
Day Two: 1,536 miles. Ten states. 990,000 strokes. Baton Rouge.
Day Three: 1,524 miles. Ten states. 980,000 strokes. Baton Rouge.
Day Four: 1,500-plus miles. Ten states. Too many strokes. Baton Rouge.

Day Five: Way too many miles. Way too many strokes. Way too far to Baton Rouge.

My daily ritual was in desperate need of revision.

Andy traveled ahead of me in the "channel" — my path down the River. Cone-shaped red buoys (nuns) on the left and square-shaped green buoys (cans) on the right defined the commercial lane of this busy, working River. Every day Andy folded his 6'5" frame into his small inflatable boat equipped with an eight-horsepower motor. A pillow-like flotation device cushioned him from the hard bench. Like a skilled race-car driver, Andy guided me on our winding course. He cut off the curves by traveling from nuns to cans and cans to nuns, maneuvering his boat in the straightest line. A Power Squadrons escort boat followed about fifty feet behind me. Captain and crew kept us safe by waving their arms and yelling at oncoming traffic.

We shared the channel, at times less than the width of a football field, with towboats pushing long chains of flatbed barges bringing goods up and down the River. Sometimes we passed as many as fifteen barges, hooked by large cables, strung together like railroad cars. Andy negotiated our way around yachts, paddle wheelers, and crisscrossing Jet Skis, part of the chaos of our crowded path. Late morning on the third day, I followed him to mile marker 785, four miles south of Red Wing, Minnesota. As I pulled my head up to keep Andy in sight, I spotted a large body of water in front of me.

"What is that?" I asked.

Lake Pepin stared me down.

Nature has good moods — sunny seventy-five degree days, brilliant orange sunsets, and majestic oceans — and bad moods — blizzards, hurricanes, and Lake Pepin.

Many people who have experienced the breathtaking beauty of eagles congregating on the spectacular bluffs that tower over the lake or skied its inviting waters (like Ralph Samuelson, who in 1922 invented waterskiing on the lake) would argue with my judgment of Minnesota's Lake Pepin.

It's located seventy miles south of Minneapolis, where the Chippewa River flows into the Mississippi. The faster-flowing current of the Chippewa deposits its sediment as it hits the slower-moving Mississippi, forming a delta that causes a perfect natural dam. The result is a lake — twenty-two miles long and two miles wide — in the *middle* of the Mississippi.

The channel cut directly through the center of the lake. Four-foot waves surrounded me as far as I could see. I couldn't make out the shorelines more than a mile away in either direction. I could barely see the spectacular bluffs that rose 450-feet above the lake. The current faded and my swimming turned slow and tedious. A four-hour swim dragged on for six. My body moaned. My muscles ached. Each morning, I began where I left off the night before, only stiffer. Specks in the middle of Pepin, it was as if we were stuck in the movie, *Honey, I Shrunk the Kids*.

My few moments of fun in Pepin came when graceful bald eagles, with seven-foot wingspans, flew over my head. When I got tired or bored, I would flip over onto my back and watch as one flapped its wings once, just enough to grab a stream of air and continue in effortless circles.

"Andy, these are eagles, aren't they? I don't look bad enough for vultures to circle, do I?"

After three days of torturous swimming, Lake Pepin ended before I did. So did the first week. I longed for a day of rest. Better yet, a sunny beach in L.A.

We spent our first day off in Wabasha, Minnesota, at the oldest hotel in the state, The Anderson House, a charming country inn opened in 1856. Many of the original pieces of furniture and fixtures are still intact in this Victorian retreat.

As we finished the check-in process, our Midwestern host smiled and asked if we would like a cat with our room. Andy and I hesitated. A real cat? We said, "Sure."

Soon the bellman showed up with our bags and Mickey.

Our loaner cat was a pudgy, calico-colored, longhaired house cat that slept all day and jumped from bed to bed all night. Mickey became my friend and confidant. I lay in bed on our first day of rest, absentmindedly petting him while I studied the map.

"Mickey, look. Here is Minneapolis and here is where we are now. I've been swimming for six days and I've only gone ninety miles. I'm exhausted. How am I going to take that outrageous number of strokes that I've stopped counting? What am I going to do?"

Mickey stared back at me with big curious eyes and then closed them, nuzzling his head deeper into the pillow. I watched him purr, contentment painting a slight smile on his face. The luscious soft bedding consumed him.

In my exhausted state, I'd had a dream. In my dream, I entered a white room. The walls were painted a soft white, the floors were covered with a soft white carpet, and soft music played in the background. In the middle of the room stood a big white bed, heaped with a fluffy white comforter, white satin sheets, and an enormous white pillow. I walked straight to the bed, lay down, and fell sleep. All night I dreamt of sleeping.

"Mickey, what if I make getting to the next bed my goal?" Mickey stretched, eyes closed, turned over onto his side and kept sleeping. I interpreted this to mean that it was a great idea.

All too soon, I had to say goodbye to Mickey and the luxury of The Anderson House to continue the journey. Time to try my new scheme. When I had thirty minutes left to swim and my muscles ached, I imagined myself nestled on a cushy white bed, on top of satin sheets, engulfed in a thick heavy comforter with my head on a giant pillow. I forgot about my tired legs and aching triceps. My imaginary bed kept me swimming. After awhile, it scared me that the image of a Motel 6 flowered bedspread was enough.

For a little while, it worked — Mickey and the beds kept me going. But, like many short-term goals, eventually this one got old. I had to find something new.

I looked ahead — my next target was hard to miss.

Dams are a familiar sight for people traveling the River north of St. Louis. In 1930, the U.S. Army Corps of Engineers was commissioned by Congress to design and build twenty-nine dams along the Upper Mississippi (between Minneapolis and St. Louis). Their purpose is to maintain the water level in the channel at nine feet. The dams raise the natural six-foot depth of the River by three feet, allowing shipping companies to use large barges to carry grain, petroleum, and manufactured goods to market. River traffic crosses from one side of the dam to the other through a lock, an elevator-like structure built into the side of the dam and controlled by a lockmaster.

About 500 feet before each dam, Andy and I climbed into our escort boat. Most of the lockmasters knew about my Swim and emerged from their tinted-windowed enclave, stationed on top of the lock, to greet us.

"How's it going?" or "Be careful, we've got a storm coming." Then a friendly wave before electronically opening the lock's two large metal doors.

This ten-minute door-opening procedure enabled us to enter the football-field-size space. Once we were safely in, the doors closed. The lockmaster adjusted the water level inside. We descended the equivalent of one to five stories in about five minutes, until the water level in the lock was equal to that on the other side of the dam. With a final wave and "Good luck," the lockmaster opened the doors on the opposite side letting us exit to continue our journey.

About twenty-six miles separates the dams. It turned out to be a perfect two-day swim distance. On the first day, with the gentle help of the current, I would stroke fourteen miles with relative ease. The second day was more difficult.

Upstream of each dam, backed-up water forms a "pool," a misnomer — obnoxiously large lake is more accurate. From a swimming standpoint, pools — as large as nine miles long and five miles wide — are sheer hell. The channel zigzags across these blobs of stagnant water and the current disappears, just as it did in Lake Pepin. I could see a dam in front of me, but knew it was hours away. I dreaded the pools.

Although I had a love/hate relationship with the lock and dam system, it served me well. I would watch as the two-story concrete barrier became larger and larger, beckoning me to swim faster. I listened for the dam's warning horns, growing louder, encouraging me to keep stroking.

For three hundred miles, getting to the next dam proved to be a powerful goal. The final lock — my greatest reward.

# LESSON #5
## Adjust Your Goals

A lofty dream can become overwhelming. The finish line may seem as if it's miles away. When this happens, instead of tossing aside your ultimate dream, alter your immediate goals — the stepping-stones that move you toward your destination.

Experiment. Decide what goals are working and keep them; abandon those that aren't. Try breaking a larger goal into smaller pieces (the next stop, the next section completed, or the next level of achievement) and then string the pieces together. Attach rewards to your goals to entice you to complete them.

Use your new stepping-stones to bring you closer to your dream.

**Keep what works; abandon what doesn't.** *Even with the most sophisticated plan, it's impossible to imagine how every aspect of your dream will unfold. You may spend hours setting up a home office and then find you get more accomplished working at a local bookstore. Most likely, your major goals will not change; the smaller goals leading up to your dream may.*

I had a pre-Swim fantasy of standing on a riverbank with cameras flashing and reporters yelling questions at me about my journey, my dad, and MS. When I visualized this picture, reporters had arrived at the right place at the right time as if by magic. No phone calls. No press releases. Somehow, they heard about the Swim and came in droves. My mom, who focused her energies on the media, will attest that this was true fantasy.

When we devised our plan, our PR goals included enlisting the help of a national PR firm. Before we found the professionals we wanted, my mom jumped in to help.

With no formal training in PR, she had never heard of a press release and knew nothing about the standard methods of pitching a story. But that didn't stop her. She thought people would be intrigued by the Swim and was sure producers and editors would want to cover it.

She naively picked up the phone and called television and radio stations and newspapers and with a mother's sincerity said, "Hi, I have a wonderful story for you. Have you heard about the young man swimming the Mississippi River for his dad? Well, he's my son."

She learned that no one has the nerve to hang up the phone on a mom. Everyone would at least listen to her pitch. With a foot in the door, she could help anyone realize how happy they (and their audience) would be if they covered the story.

Her hard work paid off in an unexpected way when she received a phone call from Ken Keen. Ken had been asked to get in touch with us by his boss, the vice president of sales and marketing, who had heard about the Swim from his boss, the chief executive officer, who had heard about it from his boss, the chairman of the board. A half a world away in China on a business trip, the chairman had flipped to CNN International on his hotel TV and watched the kickoff. He wanted to know more.

We soon learned the name of the Ken's company, Biogen, Inc. We knew who they were. By coincidence, my dad was taking their drug, Avonex, one of only three FDA-approved medications for MS. These weekly shots were working miracles for him by slowing the progression of his disease.

With a phone call, Biogen became our single-largest corporate sponsor. Not only did they make a generous donation to MS research, but they also became one of our most helpful supporters.

With my mom's continued success, we dubbed her the "PR Goddess," abandoned our search for a "real" PR professional, and found a new way to achieve our PR goals.

**String smaller goals together.** *Two words can start a book. Add three hundred more and you have a page. Ten pages and now you have your first chapter. Put enough of these stepping-stones together and suddenly, you have a large dream.*

I learned the value of goal-stringing at a young age — in Mrs. Cashion's fourth grade class at Westminster Day School. Every year her students put on a play. Hundreds attend — the other grades, teachers, parents, and friends. It's big time when you're a fourth-grader. My year, the play was *Pinocchio*.

My classmates and I huddled around Mrs. Cashion waiting for our roles. Casting was straightforward. No auditioning. Parts were assigned by the teachers who made their decisions based on the "best fit" method.

"Nick, you're playing Stromboli, the evil Italian actor."

I'd be the villain of the show who kidnaps and tries to sell Pinocchio. That suited me fine.

*Pinocchio* was a musical. The Stromboli role meant about ten minutes on stage. Although I didn't have to sing (we lip-synched the words to our songs), for five of those minutes I would be dancing. Even at nine, I thought of myself as too uncoordinated to dance.

Not only would I be dancing, I would be dancing alone. No one else…just me…on stage…dancing alone…no way. I wasn't happy, but I wanted to be a part of the play, so I decided to do it.

Rehearsals began at school, but I needed more help to pull this off. Every day, I came home from school and grabbed the *Pinocchio* record. My mom helped me make up a dance that fit the music and then showed me how to learn it by breaking it into sections.

Kick, step — right. Kick, step — left. Turn, turn. I practiced the first part of the dance in my parents' large bedroom over and over and over. I finally got the hang of keeping time with the music. I even started to enjoy myself.

The next part took another week of practicing. Step left, step right, turn left twice. I learned each piece of the dance. Finally one day, my mom helped me put it all together.

When the big day arrived, I felt ready to dance with the Rockettes at Radio City Music Hall. I wasn't nervous or scared — just excited. I looked the part with a shiny red cape, a glittery sequined cane (that I still have), and a black satin top hat. A black handlebar mustache, painted on my upper lip, completed the look.

I strode out on stage with confidence, as I imagined Stromboli would. I said my lines as loudly as I could. Then my music, piped into the room over the speakers, filled the air. I lip-synched and danced.

Step, kick, step, kick, turn, turn. My feet moved without my help — in perfect time with the music. They flew fast and furiously. I was doing the best dance I had ever done. As the song ended, I spun, went down on one knee and stretched my arms toward the audience. This dramatic move that I practiced for days on end paid off; they cheered wildly.

As they began to quiet down, I stood, crossed my arms over my puffed-up chest and again opened them toward the audience. They loved it. They cheered, enticing me to do it again…and again…and again. Every time they started to quiet down, I opened my arms and added another bow. My parents said I bowed about as long as I'd danced. Everyone laughed and cheered and laughed some more. From one step to this. Who would have thought?

**Attach a reward to your goal.** *Completing a goal, in and of itself, is a reward. But it never hurts to sweeten the outcome. A long massage after a seventy-five mile bike ride will entice you to pedal a bit faster. A vacation at the beach may prod you to get in shape. Attaching something enticing to your goal keeps you moving toward it.*

Swimming ten thousand strokes burns over 9,000 calories — the equivalent of eighteen Big Macs, four large pizzas, or twenty pieces of fried chicken. I started the Swim weighing 215 pounds, but quickly lost weight. Burning so many calories every day, I was losing ten pounds a month. Andy started calling me "Twig Boy."

The gnawing emptiness of my stomach, which often consumed my thoughts, helped me craft an incentive for completing my daily swim. I stroked during my two-hour sets, knowing that when I finished there would be something to eat waiting for me. I felt at one with our hunter/gatherer ancestors whose lives revolved around food. I sometimes imagined myself standing on shore holding a soggy sign: "WILL SWIM THE MISSISSIPPI RIVER FOR FOOD."

Each day, I imagined a different treat for myself.

On an all-around sluggish morning, when my arms felt like they weighed a thousand pounds and my legs dragged behind me like dead weight, I pictured the reward in store for me — graham crackers. More than anything else in this world, I craved the sweetness of honey and molasses that only a graham cracker can provide. For fifteen minutes, I mentally broke each one along its perforations. Slowly, I placed the perfect rectangles on my tongue. Mmmm. I savored the thought of the first taste of this treat melting in my mouth. Slowly, slowly, I swallowed.

When I boarded the escort boat for my next break, I tore the place apart looking for graham crackers. None. Anywhere.

The image of the Nabisco box with all those crackers tightly wrapped to keep their flavor kept me swimming. I was like a crazed animal. I couldn't wait to get to our next shore stop where only the Wal-Mart checkout line stood between me and my prey.

I consumed the entire box.

## MAKE IT HAPPEN

### LESSON #5: *Adjust Your Goals*

If your big dream begins to feel overwhelming, it's time to fine-tune your goals. These activities will help you modify your goals and make them seem more manageable.

1. List the goals that are moving your dream ahead. Which ones are holding it back? Comparing the lists, ask yourself:
    - *Why are some working and others not?*
    - *How can I modify the goals that aren't working?*
    - *What do I need to keep?*
    - *What do I need to throw away?*

2. Think about a time when you strung smaller goals together to learn something new or meet a deadline.
    - How did you choose the smaller goals?
    - Did stringing them together make the larger goal seem more doable?
    - Did you feel less overwhelmed?
3. Pick a goal from your plan and attach a reward to it. What would keep you moving forward?
   Suggestions:
    - Have a party.
    - Take a day off.
    - Go on vacation.
    - Spend more time with your family.
    - Buy something just for yourself.

*We are all worms, but I do believe
that I am a glowworm.*

WINSTON CHURCHILL

# 6

# I THINK I CAN, I THINK I CAN, I KNOW I CAN
## Discover Self-Confidence

*With unlimited self-confidence, anything is possible.*
*An unwavering belief in yourself, your talents, and your strengths*
*enables you to complete your dream. Confidence allows you*
*to turn "you can't" into "I did." You will be tested,*
*but when you forge ahead your confidence soars.*

~

Andy and I looked at each other. No need to speak; we knew what we had to do. A miscommunication had left our new escort thirty miles downstream. We bobbed in the water north of La Crosse, Wisconsin. With only two weeks to complete 200 miles, I had long days of swimming ahead of me. If we had any hope of making it to the celebration planned for us in Burlington, Iowa, on July 11, we had to keep going. Alone.

Before entering its unknown waters, I wanted to know everything possible about swimming the Mississippi. I talked with people living along the River — from Minnesota to Louisiana. One told me about the pollution, another said strong whirlpools in their area would suck me under, another cautioned about violent storms. Most agreed, "You'll never make it." They all slipped the word *impossible* into the conversation at least once. Undaunted by the dire warnings, I held on to my belief that I was destined to swim this River.

Everyone feared the River's traffic — barges, pleasure boaters, water skiers, and Jet Skis. Many people told us these would be bigger obstacles than anything Mother Nature could throw at us.

"They won't see you. They'll run you down."

I brushed off their words. What's the big deal? How hard can it be to see a swimmer? I'll keep my distance, they'll keep theirs, and we'll share the vast waterway. Admittedly, I was naive. I had never seen the River, and my only boating experience was waterskiing on a family vacation in Hawaii.

After a week, watching our Power Squadrons escorts use their larger boats, radios, and sirens to capture the attention of other craft, I figured it out. It was easy to spot us…if anyone looked. Swimmers and small craft are a rare sight on the Mississippi. No one is looking.

When the escort boat followed behind us, other boaters knew we were in the water. We felt relatively safe. A boating disaster was not an issue Andy and I dwelled on…until La Crosse, Wisconsin.

"Ready, Andy?"

"Go for it," he replied.

Four miles north of Lock and Dam 7, I zipped up my wetsuit and jumped off the side of the dinghy, knowing it would send Andy spinning.

"Damn, Nick. Can't you just get into the water like a normal person?"

With two tugs on the starter cord, his motor hummed and he pulled ahead. I dipped my face into the cool River, stretched my body, and stroked long gliding strokes through the glassy water.

By ten o'clock, the balmy morning with its gentle cool breeze gave way to upper eighty-degree temperatures and stagnant humidity. Andy baked. The sun in the cloudless sky beamed its rays directly on his already red ears. Sweat dripped from his bushy hair. He swatted hungry flies off his legs and fanned himself with a floppy hat. I felt bad for him. He looked miserable. I kept swimming, eager to end the day for both of us.

The dam ahead grew larger and larger. My thoughts turned to getting through the next lock by ourselves. Mere feet from the entrance, Andy waved, signaling me to climb aboard his boat.

"Let's try it," he said.

We approached the giant doors of our sixth lock. If we'd had an escort, we would have been tethering Andy's dinghy to the larger boat, then climbing inside to drink a gallon of Gatorade, relax and cool off, leaving the locking procedure to our escorts. I picked up our hand-held marine radio, turned to channel fourteen, and said in my most nautical voice:

"This is the *Mississippi Swim for Multiple Sclerosis*. We'd like to lock through."

We listened for our okay to enter. Nothing.

I called again, hoping the lockmaster would tell us how long our wait would be. Nothing.

For an hour, we floated in circles in the blistering sun, calling, waiting, and listening to the silence of the radio.

"What's with the lockmaster?" I asked. Until this time, the lockmasters had all been helpful. Why weren't we getting an answer?

"Do you think it's working?" Andy asked, tapping the radio.

"I hope so. It'll be a long day without it."

Finally, the lock doors opened. A massive tow pushing nine barges appeared. Another call to the lockmaster. No response.

"Let's go," Andy said pulling the cord to start his engine. Seizing the opportunity, we made a break for it.

As the tow crawled out through the heavy metal doors, we

inched forward. Andy, now proficient in piloting the dinghy, maneuvered us as far away from the barge and its undertow as the twenty-foot space separating us would allow. Alone, in the expanse of the lock, the doors closed. Silence echoed around us. A tiny speck in the middle of the giant elevator, we began our descent.

Like a rubber ducky in a bathtub when the drain is opened, we rode the water level down eight feet until the doors on the other side opened. A horn blew signaling it was safe to leave.

A tow entering to take its barge load upstream stared us down. Goliath wasn't expecting to encounter David in an eleven-foot inflatable. He left us little room to pass. With finesse, Andy negotiated the space between us and the barge and work tow (a smaller boat used to help maneuver the barge into the lock). Closer than we had ever been to these monstrous vessels, I gazed up in awe at the mass of steel towering four stories into the sky. Andy steered us away from the wakes it created.

We were emptied into a new world — an Alice in Wonderland of hundreds of cabin cruisers (most thirty-foot or larger), speedboats, and Jet Skis crisscrossing the channel. I think the 100-degree Saturday had brought out every boater in western Wisconsin.

"What do you think?" I asked Andy.

"We can do it," he answered.

My thoughts exactly.

I jumped into the water. Within minutes, a boat in the distance came flying toward us. Andy sprang to his feet, his arms high over his head. He waved his long arms back and forth, faster and faster. If the boaters couldn't see a swimmer, maybe they would spot the flailing motion of a tall figure in the middle of the channel.

At the last second, the captain made a sharp right turn and missed us by less than twenty feet. His wake sent water crashing over my head, and I gulped a mouthful. Andy sat quickly to avoid being flipped into the chilly water. Seconds later, another boat approached, then turned spewing its black, pungent exhaust into our faces. I coughed and Andy yelled. Would this day ever end?

To our left and right, speedboats raced each other. Sleek cigarette boats sped forty to fifty miles per hour with no apparent destination in mind. The crafts' blaring music filled the air. Fifteen-year-old Jet Skiers jumped the choppy waves left by the larger boats. Downtown La Crosse, our stop for the day and nearest escape from the mass of boating madness, was four miles ahead.

Andy flipped through the marine radio channels.

"There's a swimmer in the water," he said again and again. His voice grew louder and louder. Nothing happened.

As I swam, the underwater noise from engines increased to a deafening roar as boats approached. Andy placed a few more calls before tossing the radio aside. For most of the next hour he stood waving and yelling. The city was still nowhere in sight.

I stopped to take my last break. Fear turned into anger. "This is ridiculous. They're paying no attention."

My usually mild-mannered brother transformed into Godzilla before my eyes. "Why are they waving at us? And smiling? Can't they see they're coming too close?"

We moaned and complained. Break time over — we continued on.

I began my last swimming set for the day a short distance from the interstate bridge marking the northern edge of the city of La Crosse. The bridge looked like any of the dozens of bridges we had encountered so far, except the pylons seemed closer to each other than usual.

When Andy guided me under a bridge, he purposefully stayed just right of center in our traffic lane — away from the currents that swirl in unpredictable motion around the pylons. This bridge had limited space for us to safely pass. We both hoped we could make it through without encountering oncoming boat traffic.

Caught up in swimming the last mile, I didn't notice the thirty-foot cabin cruiser heading toward us at full speed. When

I finally looked up, it was too late. I was trapped in its wake and being thrown toward the posts. Unable to control my destiny, I prayed I would land before being smashed into the concrete slab within feet of me.

The wave plopped me down and released me less than six feet from a sudden end to my Swim. Suddenly, I was caught in the flow of water that surrounded the pylon. I could feel the funky currents tug at my legs — trying to pull me under.

I couldn't let my Swim end this way. I kicked hard and pulled every stroke with fervor until I got back to Andy and safer water. We'd survived another few terrifying moments.

"Look, Andy," I yelled.

Downtown La Crosse was now, finally, within eyesight.

# LESSON #6
## *Discover Self-confidence*

An unwavering belief in yourself and your abilities allows you to conquer what others tell you is too difficult or impossible.

Confidence is easy to build. It soars when you face a challenge and win, or when you confront your biggest fear. You can draw from past experiences that make you proud or pat yourself on the back when you accomplish something new.

Intentionally increase your self-confidence — without it, your dream *will* be impossible.

**Draw from past experience.** *You have already accomplished something extraordinary in your personal life or work life. It's this accomplishment that allows you to say, "I can make my dream come true because I have already..." Remember something you've done that makes you proud.*

In the summer between my freshman and sophomore years in college, I took a screenwriting class at UCLA. It was one of the best summers of my life. I spent two hours a week in class and forty hours a week at the beach learning the finer points of bodysurfing. At the end of two glorious months of sun and surf, my dad flew to Los Angeles and picked me up to drive to San Francisco, where we were meeting my mom and Andy.

Before leaving Southern California, I wanted one last adventure — a bungee jump in the mountains. To my surprise, my dad agreed to drive me to a secret (and illegal) jump site on our way north, an hour and a half outside of L.A. Driving the winding and twisting roads, we worked our way up to our destination, a bridge overlooking a magnificent canyon 250 feet below. We climbed higher and higher until we reached the concrete structure that would serve as the base for the jump. We pulled up to a large dirt parking lot on the far side of the bridge, where I joined the group of people milling around waiting for instructions.

Before long, three well-muscled, tanned California types demonstrated how to put on the harnesses that would keep us from free-falling to a sudden death in the canyon below. I listened intently.

After an orientation explaining (in relatively little detail) the equipment we were using and the mechanics of the jump, we lined up on the bridge to await our turn. I noticed my dad standing behind me, looking a bit pale. I knew he probably wouldn't have jumped for a million dollars, but, like always, he was enjoying my adventure and cheering me on.

Lookouts stood on each side of the bridge in case police joined the party. If they gave the signal — a boisterous yell — everyone would pretend they were throwing a Frisbee, sightseeing, or whatever else you do on a bridge in the mountains overlooking a perfect bungee-jumping canyon. This sport was illegal at the time, and nobody wanted a hefty fine for a three-minute rush of pleasure.

One after another, terrified adventure-seekers stood on the bridge, climbed over the guardrail, and did their best swan dive over the edge. Reaching the bottom, they flew back within ten feet of where they started and fell again.

Cheering for each new jumper kept my mind occupied. Suddenly, it was my turn. My heart rate soared. I made my way over to the edge of the bridge to be hooked to the all-important bungee cord, giving new meaning to the phrase "putting your life on the line." The bungee master attached two cords to my harness. The first would stretch to bounce me up and down on my joy ride. The second was a backup in case the first one broke. A comforting thought. Combined, they weighed about ten pounds, and could support up to 2,000 pounds. Okay — that's far more than my mere 200-pound body.

"Your turn, Nick. Climb over the guardrail and take it all in." Easy to say for the bungee guru making his hundredth dive that day.

Face to face with the ultimate "trust fall," I did as instructed. I felt the weight of the bungee cord pulling me down toward the jagged rocks of the dried-up creek bed.

Silence.

"Ready, Nick?"

"Ready."

Then the counting began.

"Three...Two...One...Bungee!"

On "bungee," I spread my arms emulating Greg Louganis. Ah — the perfect swan dive. Or so I thought. I reached toward the rocks and trees beneath me. Jumping with too much enthusiasm, I over-rotated and did a three-quarter flip. I ended at the full stretch of the cord with my back to the ground. No big deal — until I bounced back up toward the lifeline and hit my face. I wore the nickel-sized "bungee burn" on my chin with pride.

Once I reached the bottom of the jump, the fun began. Falling was terrifying. Being thrown back up into the air at a hundred miles an hour was exhilarating. Not even the best Six Flags roller coaster could match the rush of this ride. At the top, I realized I had to fall again. Oh, no! I had to fall again. At least this time, I knew the trip back up would be my reward.

After ten bounces, I came to a halt one hundred feet off the ground. Sitting back in my harness, I waited to grab the rope that would bring me back up. I "hung out" in complete silence, a rainbow of nature surrounding me, the thrill of the experience tingling within me. I wanted this moment to last forever.

Back at school in the fall, I used the bungee experience as my inspiration. I had jumped off a bridge and survived. Now, I could do anything. How hard could a history test be? I had jumped off a bridge. How hard could a swim practice be? I had jumped off a bridge. How hard could anything be? I had jumped off a bridge.

**Face your biggest fears.** *Nothing builds confidence more than facing your fears. Experience the incredible feeling of pride that comes when you challenge fear and win. If you're scared of heights, go skydiving. If you're terrified to be in front of a crowd, sing on stage. If you're afraid of change, try a new hairstyle.*

I jumped into the water just south of Lock and Dam 15, about a half-mile up the River from La Claire Park in Davenport, Iowa, and stroked toward the roar that was growing louder and louder. The noise drowned out the hum of the motor on Andy's boat. I rounded a bend to find thousands of blues fans standing against the railing waving and yelling indistinguishable words. Seconds earlier the band stopped playing and over the loudspeaker an announcement: "Ladies and gentlemen, if you look to the River, you will soon see Nick Irons, the man swimming the Mississippi."

A radio station, WXLP (97-X), hosted the Mississippi Valley Blues Festival. This Quad Cities' (Davenport and Bettendorf, Iowa, Rock Island and Moline, Illinois) yearly two-day event draws 10,000 fans who park their plastic lawn chairs, spread their blankets, and open their coolers to enjoy blues at the band shell in the park.

For the entire month of June, the 97-X shock jocks, Matt and Homey, plugged the event. They ended promotions with the words "and a special appearance by Nick Irons, the man swimming the Mississippi River." What an incredible opportunity. A huge group of potential supporters loomed out there. And besides, I love the blues.

Andy guided me through the maze of boats anchored in the River, their occupants enjoying the blues show. He pulled alongside a houseboat, exchanged a few words with the captain, and then motioned for me to climb aboard. The owners showed me to the cabin where I changed into dry clothes.

I then climbed onto the roof of the boat, grabbed the railing of the park, and swung my legs over. I felt like a rock star entering the crowd in a somewhat unconventional way. People shook my hand and slapped me on the back. "We're so excited you're here." I blushed as a woman whistled at me.

The crowd suddenly parted for a security officer in a golf cart.

"Welcome to Davenport, Mr. Irons. If you come with me, I'll take you on stage." I felt like the Pope in the "PopeMobile" as we cut through the crowd.

On stage, Matt and Homey welcomed me and introduced me to the crowd. I stood silently for a second gazing over the expansive lawn, looking into faces of all those people.

They handed me the microphone…and it hit me…

5,000 people…

10,000 staring eyes.

My knees trembled, my hands dripped with sweat, my heart felt like it would pound out of my chest and fall onto the stage. All these people were waiting to hear me say something interesting, or inspiring, or at least as entertaining as the Blues Festival.

Studies show that the average American's greatest fear in life is speaking in public. We're more afraid of public speaking than spiders, snakes, small spaces, or clowns. More afraid than dying a slow, painful death. I never understood why — until I stood on stage at the Mississippi Valley Blues Festival.

No one had warned me that they would want a speech. I stood in excruciating silence. Time stopped. I was sure my heart would, too. Paramedics would have to carry off my limp body. My Swim wouldn't end in the Mississippi, but on stage. My death certificate would read, "Cause of Death: stage fright." Those were the longest five seconds of my life.

Think, Nick, think. You can do this. You spoke to 1,000 times as many people when you were on *Good Morning America*. You can do this. You know what to say. Just tell them your story. You've been doing it for five weeks. You can do this.

Just do it. *Now. Right now.* I took a huge breath.

"Hello, Davenport!" I yelled in my favorite rock-star voice.

The system amplified my words, making them louder than a jet engine. Oh, no — more pressure — everyone for blocks would hear me.

Looking over at Matt and Homey, I somehow managed the words, "Five weeks ago, I learned that you two were hosting the Mississippi Valley Blues Festival. It sounded so great, I decided to swim here."

The crowd went wild…screaming…clapping…cheering.

I laughed. That wasn't so bad.

"But seriously . . ." I took a long pause. No longer gripped by fear, I looked out and drank in the crowd of smiling faces.

I told my story — why I was swimming — a bit about MS and

my dad. By the end of these few minutes, I was actually thinking about what I was going to say before I said it, and best of all — I was still alive.

**Go forward with blind faith in yourself.** *In pursuing your dream, you have to believe that you can face any circumstance and succeed. Believe in yourself and your abilities, and you'll amaze yourself. Jump in with both feet and never look back.*

At seventeen, with unshakable confidence, my mom's father, Grandpa Marra, boarded a trans-Atlantic passenger ship in Naples, Italy, and set sail for the United States. Greeted by the Statue of Liberty, filled with hopes and dreams, he left the boat and hailed a cab. He spoke no English and now he was alone in the largest city he had ever seen. An Italian-American taxi driver picked him up.

From the moment he stepped into the cab, my grandfather's contagious personality amused the cabbie. He chuckled at my grandpa's enthusiasm, liked his zest for adventure, and admired his courage to start a new life in a new country. He decided to share his love of New York City with the young adventurer.

He brought him to the top of the Empire State Building, showed him Wall Street, Broadway, and Greenwich Village. They ate pasta with the cabbie's friends (most from the "Old Country") in Little Italy and shared stories about their homeland.

After a whirlwind day filled with New York experiences, his new friend gave my grandfather a piece of paper with the words he taught him in English: Hello. Thank you. How do I find…? How much does it cost? Then he dropped him off at the train station, refused payment, and sent my grandfather on his way to find relatives in Chicago and a lifelong adventure in a new land.

My grandfather lived his life with passion. He approached each new day with the excitement of a child opening a birthday gift. It didn't matter that he was thousands of miles away from a loving family and the security of a known life. His belief in himself was all he needed. He learned English, married, raised a family, and started J. Thomas Marra Custom Tailors, the business he always dreamt of owning.

After he retired, he moved to Oklahoma City to be close to the family he adored. He stopped by our house each morning and brought sugar doughnuts, optimism, and his love of life. I'll always be grateful that he gently passed these gifts on.

## MAKE IT HAPPEN

### LESSON #6: *Discover Self-confidence*

The more self-confidence you have, the more likely you are to complete your dream successfully. These activities will help you uncover the confidence you already have and will challenge you to build even more.

1. Write down the three personal accomplishments that make you most proud.
   - What did you achieve?
   - What obstacles did you face?
   - How did you overcome those obstacles?
   - How did you feel when you were successful?

2. Do something that puts your confidence to the test. Here are some ideas:
   - At a gathering, introduce yourself to a complete stranger.
   - Ask a good-looking man or woman to dinner.
   - Ask your boss for a raise.
   - Speak in public.
   - Skydive.

2. Think of your biggest fear. How can you safely face it? Make plans to do it.

*Wheresoever you go, go with all your heart.*

CONFUCIUS

# 7

# KEEP THE FIRE BURNING
## Find Your Motivation

*There will be times in the pursuit of your dream when you
want to quit. There may be times every day when you want to quit.
Without something powerful to keep you going, in good times
and bad, you'll find an excuse to say "enough."
You may have to remind yourself, from time to time,
why you're working so hard to make your dream come true.*

~

I loved the Mississippi on glassy days. Calm and peaceful, the River was mine. I gained a respect for it when storms produced four-foot waves that rose into the air then crashed and tangled with churning currents. When water, swirling in unpredictable motion, tossed me from side to side. That was when I understood the meaning of "Mighty Mississippi."

Life on the River was primal. Andy and I were closer to nature than we had ever been — and closer than I want to be again. Because my dad's idea of "camping" was a Marriott Hotel, Andy and I had never been on a real in-the-woods-sleep-on-the-ground-with-the-bugs camping trip. Mother Nature's prominence in our daily lives surprised us.

I had always thought of the weather report as a space-filler between the news and sports. Now, information about air temperature, wind advisories, and flood stages took on new meaning. Each morning we searched the TV for the local forecast. Often the broadcast came from a larger city hundreds of miles away — sometimes helpful, sometimes not.

"Seventy degrees today and overcast. Winds from the north at fifteen miles per hour," the weatherperson might inform us.

For Andy, that was a code for "your red, blistered ears will have a day to heal." For me, it meant a calm swim with just enough current to help me complete my twelve to fourteen miles in four hours instead of five.

Because we covered so many miles over such a long period of time, we had a taste of everything. We endured temperatures that dipped into the thirties or soared over 100 degrees. Sweat dripped when the humidity hovered around ninety percent. We battled winds gusting to forty or fifty miles per hour and thunderstorms that slithered like a snake out of nowhere and left just as quickly. Floods swelled the river. They filled it with dead trees and logs that blocked my path. Droughts robbed me of strong currents to push me forward. The quality of our lives and our moods often centered around weather conditions.

It didn't matter where we were geographically; I paid attention to weather reports in other parts of the country as well. Directly or indirectly, water from one third of the country flows into the Mississippi. Melting snows from Chicago swell the River's summer flow. When it rains in Ohio, the currents intensify in Memphis. Storms in Nebraska, North Dakota, and South Dakota raise the water table south of St. Louis.

Two-hundred-thirty miles into our journey, I woke up at 6:30 a.m. in Guttenberg, Iowa, to the bang of trees slamming against the roof of our three-room motel. In my daze, I thought we were in the middle of a thunderstorm. What I heard was only the wind in front of the approaching storm.

After breakfast, we left the motel to meet our Power Squadrons escort for the day. As we drove down the steep hill to the marina, the howling wind pounded on the windows of the car. I scanned the sky searching for signs of the lurking storm and tried to catch a glimpse of what nature had in store for us.

Most of our tag-team boaters donated a day or two to our journey; this was day four for brothers-in-law Dave Douglas and Norm Kohl, who had traveled ninety miles from Cedar Rapids, Iowa, to help us travel safely down the River.

Norm, tall and large and in his early sixties, is a man of few words. As a union pipe fitter, Norm had installed fire sprinkler systems in many Cedar Rapids buildings. He took pride in his work. He's the kind of man you can trust to do his best — all the time.

Dave's well-tanned skin and athletic build defied his fifty-seven years. Early retirement from his thirty-three-year job at the defense contractor Rockwell/Collins allowed him to spend long-overdue free time caring for his boat, the *Misty Blue*. He showered her with attention as if she were a member of his family. He waxed and polished her deck, pulled zebra muscles from her propeller, and kept her engine humming. With Norm and Dave, Andy and I felt safe.

We approached the dock and spotted Dave sprinting as fast as a twenty-year-old, flagging down a white Jeep Cherokee. There had been a mix-up. A Cedar Rapids TV reporter, Cary J. Hahn, a.k.a. "The Iowa Traveler," couldn't find us and was about to leave without his interview.

"He's over by the *Misty Blue!*" Dave shouted, pointing our way.

A stocky man with trademark white tennis shoes bounced out of the SUV, pen and paper in hand, and headed toward us at the water's edge. "The Iowa Traveler" was legendary. The local celebrity was famous for covering a chili cook-off in Ames one day, a 4th of July parade in Dubuque the next, followed by a biplane exhibit in Cedar Rapids. When human-interest stories developed anywhere in the state, you could count on Cary J. to be there. I was his next story.

Dave finally joined us. "Hey, guys."

His face seemed incongruent — his warm smile mixed with deer-in-the-headlights eyes that kept circling from our faces to the River and back. He was making me nervous.

I looked past his boat and caught sight of his dread. The River was white — from our dock to the tree bank on the other side. The wind, forecasted at a steady thirty miles per hour gusting to fifty or sixty, was producing four-foot waves. Water crashed against the dock. This was not the same river we left the night before. Was this the river people had been warning us about?

I boarded the *Misty Blue* with Dave and Norm, followed by Andy, Cary J. and his cameraman Jer Edwards. We rode to mile marker 595. Dave knew the routine. Each day we returned to the exact spot we had left the day before to begin the next leg of the journey.

As the *Misty Blue* jumped the waves, water flying over the bow, I sat on deck chairs with Cary J., answering the standard questions — How far? How many miles per day? Why are you doing this? The interview distracted me from the gusts that muffled our words and rearranged everyone's hair except mine.

We reached our starting point. Andy left the safety of Dave's larger boat to board his dinghy. His tiny craft looked even smaller caught in the middle of the clash of waves. He struggled to keep it in control as the wind whipped it back and forth.

I prepared for the swim as if everything was usual. I swung my arms in front of my body a couple of times and mumbled.

"I can do this." I stretched my left shoulder.

"Nothing's different." I stretched my right shoulder.

"Just twelve miles to swim."

I jumped into the menacing River and waves crashed over my head. I bobbed in the turbulent water. "This will be fun."

I tried to ride the waves, but they had no direction. I caught one. The next pushed me back. One slammed me from the left side, while another pounded me on the right. I was wrong. This was not fun. The only positive was the bit of drama we provided for the TV camera.

The swimming was awful. For an hour, I wasn't going anywhere. I couldn't get into a comfortable rhythm or take in a full breath of air. Worst of all, my goggles fogged up so I couldn't see anything. I pulled my head up to find Andy and some direction, but saw nothing, so I kept swimming. I tried again. Nothing. A wall of water separated us, so I didn't see him when he stopped his boat in front of me for my half-hourly break. I kept swimming…BAM…right into the side of his boat. My head snapped back, and my goggles dug deep into the bridge of my nose. I watched blood fall drop by drop into the muddy water.

I hung onto the side of Andy's boat, dazed, bloody and aching. I must have looked terrible because Andy, who had studied theater since age ten, couldn't even *act* encouraging. He looked down at me and said, "Feel like getting out?"

That was a hard question for me to answer.

Of course I want to get out. I'm sick of this. I'm sick of swimming. I'm sick of being wet seven hours a day. I'm sick of the pain. No more. I've had enough.

But then, I thought about my dad stuck on the shore, standing alone in Minneapolis. I knew he could never end his fight with MS by simply saying, "I've had enough." He could never end his pain by simply saying, "No more."

I looked up at Andy.

"If I get out now, I'll *never* get back in this damn river."

I let go of his boat and swam for another two-and-a-half hours.

# LESSON #7
## *Find Your Motivation*

Motivation keeps you going when you're ready to say, "I've had enough." You'll have an answer when you wonder why you're in the water, sweating at the gym, or rehearsing at midnight.

Look deep to uncover something persuasive to motivate you. You may discover that you have more than one reason for accomplishing your dream. That's fine. Use whatever moves you ahead and keeps you on track.

Along the way, tap into the driving forces of others to help you get to your destination.

**Discover what motivates you.** *Motivation keeps you going hour after hour, day after day. Find something powerful, fun, or inspiring to move you. It may be fame, fortune, family, friendship, or philanthropy. What makes you happy? What keeps you going when times get tough?*

After my *American Gladiators* gig, and while training for the Swim, I worked as a temp for an agency in L.A. that specialized in providing executive assistants for the entertainment industry. My assignments included stints as an assistant to executives at ABC, CBS, NBC, Warner Brothers, and Giant Records. I met some talented people and learned a lot about TV and movie production.

One morning, the agency directed me to Walt Disney Theatrical Productions. I pictured myself working for a heavy-hitting movie producer. We would be closing deals over lunch with stars.

In my best khaki pants and freshly ironed shirt, I bounced into the office eager to begin. Was I in the right place? A jungle of cubicles plastered with pictures of brightly costumed characters — a singing teakettle, armoires, and candlesticks with smiling faces — surrounded me. The office walls, papered with gigantic posters of *Beauty and the Beast*, gave me my first clue that "Theatrical," in this case, was a derivative of the word "theater" — as in Broadway — and that I wasn't in a movie executive's suite.

My boss escorted me to the "Group Sales" section, fitted me with a headset, handed me a script, and disappeared to his "executive office" around the corner. My second hint.

For the rest of that eight-hour day, I manned the phones, answering calls from church groups in Milwaukee, senior citizens in Hartford, and Tee Ball teams in Atlanta — anyone interested in purchasing ten or more tickets for the Broadway production of *Beauty and the Beast*.

It took less than two days on the job for me to lose my mind. On the morning of the third day, I was about to announce my retirement, even though I needed the money, when I answered a call from a woman in Louisville planning a celebration for her parents' fiftieth wedding anniversary. She was making arrangements to surprise her mom and dad, bringing kids and grandkids to the Big Apple on the special day.

She wanted fourteen tickets in the orchestra section. That was easy. I found fifth row, center seats and quoted her the price.

"That's more than I can afford."

"Would you like the mezzanine section?" I asked.

"My dad has cataracts and can't see very well. We really have to sit up close…shoot…I don't know what to do…shoot…let me buy twelve tickets and my husband and I and will stay at the hotel."

The thought of twelve members of her family celebrating this momentous occasion without her and her husband was too much for me.

"Let me put you on hold while I see what we can do."

I called my boss to tell him the story, confident that he would authorize a discount. Before I could finish, he told me curtly, "There's nothing we can do."

"But, they want to go as a family, and what's the point of going as a family if the father can't *see* the show?"

"Listen, Nick, there's nothing we can do."

I refused to give up. There had to be some way to pull this off. Tacked on the cubicle wall was a list of all the current promotions.

"Hello again. Let's try this. Are you a member of AAA? Do you have an American Express Card? MBNA Visa? Are your parents members of AARP? Will you be flying American Airlines anytime in the next three months?"

Each "yes" qualified her for a different promotion. We chose the best one and whittled the price. In ten minutes, she bought fourteen seats in the orchestra section for less than what she expected, and I found a way to make my job fun.

I had a new goal — to save callers as much money as humanly

possible. Someone would call thinking they would be spending $1,500 and would end up paying $1,000. If they paid $1,500, I could give them the seats they wanted, plus dinner before the show and a backstage tour. All day I offered these promotional discounts and made everyone happy. What a great job.

I learned that I like to help people, put them in a good mood, and make them laugh (and that I could never make a living in sales). I discovered something that motivates me.

**Be open to new motivations.** *On the road to your dream, you may have more than one motivation pushing you ahead. You may feel great accomplishment in producing a piece of art and, at the same time, enjoy the money you make selling it. Use each motivation to keep your dream on track.*

Every weekday during the Swim, at exactly 9:15 a.m. (East Coast time), I called the WRC-TV studios in Washington, D.C. I talked with news anchors Joe Krebs and Barbara Harrison just after Tom Kierein's weather report.

When I began doing the interviews, I had only one idea in mind — to tell people about MS and ask them to support research. I wanted people in the D.C. area to learn about the disease and know how they could help. But, as time wore on, I discovered additional motivation. These calls became my morning cup of caffeine.

For three weeks before I started swimming, I stayed with my parents in Maryland to finish last-minute details before leaving for Minneapolis. While there, I did an interview with WRC, the NBC affiliate. They produced an informative and touching five-minute story about the Swim that aired in the nation's capital a week before kickoff. Judging by the number of calls the station received, the viewers loved it and wanted to hear more. Many asked WRC to follow me as I traveled down the River.

It wasn't long before Paul, the executive producer, called my mom with a deal. If I called into their morning news program five days a week, for the entire four months of the swim, they would provide us with cell phones and airtime. Cell phones were still new and airtime expensive — especially for roaming — and the middle of the Mississippi was the ultimate roaming. We accepted their generous offer.

Each day I'd call Kenny, the assignment editor, who answered the phone with a laugh and a joke. He transferred me to the control room to talk with Michelle, the morning producer, who was more than likely stressed, but always welcoming. Before I spoke, Tom Kierein gave the weather report, often adding something about the Mississippi River. And then I talked with Barbara and Joe.

Every morning was the same. "On June 1, Nick Irons jumped into the Mississippi River...He's on the phone with us now. Nick, can you hear us?"

For three or four minutes, I talked with two old friends I had never met, as thousands of people eavesdropped. We talked about my life, both in and out of the water, about MS, and about my dad. I looked forward to these calls that became a constant link with the outside world. Even if I was in the middle of nowhere, in a town of 300 people, I knew life was going on as normal in Washington, and Joe and Barbara were always there.

Because I liked them so much, I told them things I told no one else. One morning, after an unusually hot and sticky night, without censoring, I said, "It was so hot last night, I didn't get much sleep. I just rolled around in a pool of my own sweat."

As I neared St. Louis, Joe's hometown, he arranged for his brother, Gene, to meet me under the Arch. With Gene by my side, I made my usual call to WRC. Barbara asked if Joe looked like his brother. I couldn't admit I had no idea. Living in L.A., I had never watched their show, so I said, "I'll send you pictures and let you be the judge." We all laughed, and my secret was still safe.

I knew they were concerned about my safety. When I missed a call one morning because we were out of cell-phone range, they were frantic with worry. They cared about the cause, about my family, and about me. I loved this unique friendship. The cell phones were a wonderful bonus.

**Tap into the motivation of others.** *Motivation for completing a dream is highly individual. For some people, personal accomplishment is an important motive; for others, making new friendships or achieving financial independence is a driving force. Work with other people even if their motives differ from yours. Everyone wins when you all attain your goals.*

As we neared our halfway point, my mom made her usual calls to Power Squadrons District Commanders to work out logistics (dates and times for their members to join us) and was warned, "The Lower Mississippi is a dangerous river for smaller craft."

South of St. Louis, with no locks and dams to slow the current and enormous barges ruling the waterway, pleasure boating was nonexistent. We discovered that only a handful of Power Squadrons members were brave enough to venture into the Lower River — a problem none of us had anticipated.

Our familiar black hole loomed just past Lock and Dam 27. What would we do for escort boats the last two-and-a-half months of the journey?

My mom called Dave Douglas. Maybe he had some ideas. She found we weren't the only ones with concerns. Back in Cedar Rapids, Dave, who was more familiar with the River, had been worrying about our escort problem ever since he'd left us in June. Dave and my mom brainstormed. He gave her the telephone number for the Power Squadrons Bridge Commander in Cedar Rapids. Maybe he would know someone.

"If that doesn't work, call me back," Dave said.

Two days later — still no luck. With her worries skyrocketing, she called back.

"If you found a boat, I would drive it for you," Dave offered.

She knew Dave had just taken early retirement and planned to spend his free time doing the two things that excited him the most — boating and enjoying life with his wife Judy, their three kids, five grandchildren, and a faithful companion, his dog, Misty.

"You would really do that?" My mom was touched by his offer.

"Yes," Dave said without hesitation.

My mom hung up the phone determined to find a boat. But finding boats had never been our thing. A few days and fifty phone calls later she called Dave.

"I am having a hard time getting a boat."

"Well, if we can pull all the pieces together in such a short time, I'll take my boat," Dave said.

On July 20, 1997, Dave made the decision to leave his family to spend two months traveling the Mississippi River. He would take the *Misty Blue*, his mint-condition 1988 *Bayliner 2858 Command Bridge*, meet us in St. Louis and escort us to Baton Rouge. The *Misty Blue* would become our home, and Dave, our protector. Dave had a lifelong dream to boat the length of the Mississippi River. On his way to helping the Mississippi Swim, he would have that chance.

With only three days to prepare for a trip that should have taken months to plan, Dave was busy. He bought supplies, gas cans, and back-up parts for the boat. Winegar Works Marina hoisted the boat out of the water to check the engine. Dave tracked down insurance for the Lower River, found navigational charts, and talked to other people who had traveled at least some part of the River. Judy would be his crewmate until he met up with us.

I knew that when I saw the *Misty Blue* on the horizon just north of St. Louis, I would catch a glimpse of Dave's broad smile.

"Hey, guys." He would yell.

Once again, I would feel safe.

## MAKE IT HAPPEN

### LESSON #7: *Find your Motivation*

We all have something powerful to motivate us; sometimes we have to dig deep to find it. These activities will help you discover what inspires you and keeps you going.

1. Remember a time when you used a powerful motivation to make a dream happen. If you are having trouble thinking of one, here are some ideas. Have you:
   - *lost weight?*
   - *quit smoking?*
   - *run a marathon?*
   - *had a baby?*
   - *driven cross-country?*
   - *helped a cause?*

2. Write down at least three things that motivate you to keep going. If you aren't sure, the following questions will help:
   - *Why do you go to work every morning?*
   - *Who would you be willing to fight for?*
   - *What would you be willing to die for?*
   - *What is most important in your life?*
   - *What makes you happiest?*

*The colors of a rainbow…so pretty in the sky
Are there on the faces…of people going by
I see friends shaking hands…sayin' how do you do
They're really sayin'…I love you.*

> "WHAT A WONDERFUL WORLD"
> LOUIS ARMSTRONG
> WRITTEN BY GEORGE WEISS & ROBERT THIELE

# 8

# WITH A LITTLE HELP FROM MY FRIENDS
*Put Together a Great Team*

*The success of your dream will hinge on the quality
and passion of the members of your team. Surround yourself
with people who believe in you and believe in your dream.
With loyal supporters to lend a hand or cheer you on,
accomplishing your dream is easier and more fun.*

~

Dark clouds blacked out the sun. The smell of ozone from an approaching storm filled the air. Andy clicked on his "lifejacket," a flotation belt around his waist, and tugged a few times on the lawnmower-like cord to start his motor.

Within minutes, it began to drizzle — a welcome change of pace. Andy took off his hat, leaned back in his boat, and pointed his face toward the sky. Eyes closed, he smiled in his cool shower. Before long, as the raindrops grew and made saucer-sized indentations on the water, he sat upright and zipped up his jacket.

Our escorts warned us about the incoming thunderstorm. We were on our way to a reception and press conference scheduled at the Mississippi River Museum in Dubuque, Iowa. Storm or no storm, we had to be on time. We pushed ahead.

Ever since Andy was little, he had dreamed of moving to the theater capital of the world. In New York City, surrounded by other artists, he would write plays, act with the best actors, and work under the best directors. He had been preparing for a theater career for more than half his life.

Two months before he was to graduate from Skidmore College and take that leap, I asked him to join me for four months on the Mississippi River, a half a country away from the neon of his dream. If he had any hesitation, he never let on. He postponed his future to travel the River in an 11'2" inflatable dinghy, exchanging the thrill of the Big Apple for the excitement of sleepy river towns in America's heartland. He traded center stage for backstage crewmember.

Andy came on board as a support boat driver to guide me to Baton Rouge. On the River each day, he steered me away from the debris (logs, oil cans, an occasional refrigerator) that washed into the River during storms, and from swirling eddies and anything else that could potentially hurt — or eat — me. I trusted him explicitly, even though his only training was "on-the-job."

There's a section of the River famous for its leeches. Our Power Squadrons escort for the day warned Andy that everyone who water-skis or swims in the area comes out with long, black, blood-sucking creatures attached to their bodies. Andy held on to this information tightly. Unaware of this disgusting scenario, I plunged into the water.

After two hours, my body screamed. I began to slow down. Andy knew if we stopped in the middle of leech-land, I would be easy bait. The secret to avoiding their hungry appetite and tenacious grip was to keep moving. So he used his best acting skills and shouted back to me. "You're on a roll. Why don't you keep swimming?"

Wow, Andy thought I was strong enough to keep swimming. Why not? I kept going. For an hour, he kept encouraging me to swim "just a little farther," or "just around the next bend." When I finally got out of the water, I was leech free.

Many times Andy kept me safe without telling me. He waited until I had stepped out of the water for the last time to share his first-hand knowledge of the snakes, eels, and other repulsive life forms that, with my head buried in the murky River, I happily never knew swam with me.

When I asked Andy to join me, I had no idea how much I needed him or how important he would be to the success of the Swim. From the moment we landed in Minneapolis, he began taking care of all the annoying details I hated, and that I would later be too tired to remember. Andy handled everything from getting film for the camera, to finding a place to launch the boat for kickoff, to doing the laundry — to me. (Often rescuing the billfold or glasses I left at our last motel.) He made sure I was awake and on time for media interviews. He kept us on schedule by making adjustments to our routine, and he laughed with me, keeping me sane.

Andy's passion kept the Swim on track. He had long conversations on the phone with my mom, devising ways to let people know about our efforts. He wanted people lining the shores as I swam into each new city so we could fundraise — sell MS4MS T-shirts and collect donations for research. He educated everyone he met, telling them about MS. He gave up a lot for himself to give so much to my dad, to me, my family, and other MS families.

When reporters learned that Andy and my family were an integral part of the *Mississippi Swim for Multiple Sclerosis*, they asked, "Has this Swim brought your family closer together?" I never knew how to answer that question. We loved, supported, and admired each other. Isn't that what *close* is all about? I didn't know what *closer* meant.

The storm clouds spewed as we headed toward our date with the press at the River Museum. The raindrops began to hurt as they pounded down on my bald spot. I thought it was hailing, so I stopped swimming and dove under the water to protect myself. I surfaced for a breath of air. Choppy waves, combined with a curtain of rain, erased all signs of the River.

I couldn't see our escort boat just a few feet to my side or the Dubuque River Bridge that had been in front of me a second earlier. And I couldn't see Andy. I listened for his motor, but only heard the swishing waves and kettledrum sounds of rain pounding the water around me.

While I searched for signs of him, he hit a wave and a gust of wind caught the front of his boat, blowing the bow into the air, skyward. When I finally caught a glimpse of the dinghy, it was behind me, its nose pointed to the sky — the craft perpendicular to the water. The bottom of his boat, which I had never seen before, stared at me. Through the driving rain, I could barely make out a figure tumbling out the back. Andy was heading toward the motor and its protruding propeller.

I sprinted upstream toward him trying not to think about the propeller on the unmanned boat spinning out of control. I spotted him. I could see him in the water, his blue, Gore-tex jacket clinging like a flabby extra layer of skin. I knew his shoes would deaden his feet. I stroked harder than ever and made it to his boat just as he grabbed for the side. With the dinghy now horizontal, we piled in, one after the other.

Fear turned into relief. Earlier in the day Andy had attached himself to the safety cord that cut off the motor in case of an emergency — something he usually didn't do. When he fell out of the boat, it had stopped the engine.

We decided that some things are better left unsaid, and made a pact not to tell our parents about the incident until we made it safely to Baton Rouge.

I saw just how much the Swim meant to Andy, and how far he was willing to go to make it a success. This is about as close as a relationship gets.

# LESSON #8
## *Put Together a Great Team*

Every dream needs a team. By tapping into the expertise, creativity, talents, and enthusiasm of others, you expand your ability to accomplish your dream. Even if you are the only one singing at Carnegie Hall, others along the way boosted you on stage.

When you're recruiting the perfect team, find people who are passionate about your dream. Look for those whose strengths balance your weaknesses. Allow your supporters to take on the roles they love.

Use the help of your team to make your dream a reality. Working together, everyone wins.

**Find others whose strengths complement yours.** *The perfect team will include members whose strengths vary. Some members will have knowledge and skills you may not possess. Be sure to include all personality types — from detail-oriented to creative off-the-wall. Each will have access to something that you don't — contacts, ability, or time to complete a task.*

I neared the halfway point in my journey while my parents settled into a routine at the MS4MS headquarters in Bethesda. As word spread about the Swim, the tasks my mom had undertaken multiplied out of control. Coordinating logistics — media, boat escorts, hotel rooms, fundraising, PR — consumed every moment of her 5 a.m. to 11 p.m. day, seven days a week.

The task of finding hotels willing to donate rooms often exhausted a morning. Sometimes, four or five conversations were needed to get a positive response. Because we stayed in a different hotel, in a different town, almost every night, each morning she faced another round of calls.

About two tasks away from insanity, my dad volunteered to take over the hotels. He had the one thing she didn't — extra time. Between patients at his office, he found rooms for us. He had a great time talking with people from St. Louis to Baton Rouge. Thanks to my dad who found kind people everywhere, we traveled down the River without the expense of hotels.

**Find those passionate about your dream.** *Share your dream with others and you'll discover people who are as passionate about your idea as you are — sometimes for different reasons. These people will support you and help to make your dream successful. Enlist their help.*

Pat Ricks, a fun-loving, gregarious photographer, well-known in Burlington, Iowa, for capturing high school memories in a single yearbook photo, entered our lives. After watching us on *Good Morning America*, Pat called my mom at our hotel in Minneapolis and offered to help the *Mississippi Swim for Multiple Sclerosis*.

"When Nick swims through Burlington, we'd like to throw a party that will knock your socks off."

"Great!" my mom responded.

Pat grew up along the Mississippi's shores, water-skied in its currents, and duck-hunted in its backwaters. His passion for the River was as deep as the River itself and sometimes as murky. He had seen the River's floods and devastation, but was enamored by its beauty. My Swim would become part of its history, and Pat wanted to be involved. For forty-two days before our arrival in his beloved Mississippi River town, my Swim became his obsession.

My schedule called for a "swim-in" to Burlington at 4 p.m. on July 11. Pat displayed a knack for understatement when he told us there would be "some people" to greet us when we arrived. About a mile outside of the city, in the midst of my usual routine, I spotted blue flashing lights approaching. They were perched on top of a patrol boat with "Sheriff" painted in large red letters on the side. Our escort had arrived. I flipped over to swim backstroke and wave. Shortly, the rest of the entourage showed up: a canoe, a couple of speedboats, and another sheriff's boat.

Then, the *coup de gras*, a Dragon Boat — a multi-colored wooden canoe over fifty feet long, a re-creation of a Chinese fishing boat used twenty-four hundred years ago, decorated with a dragon head, scaly body and elaborate tail. The boat housed ten paddlers on each side and a "steerer" in back. The "drummer" sat in the front, beating a cadence on a heavy wooden drum. The crew paddled one stroke to each beat.

The Dragon Boat pulled alongside of me, and the drummer changed his rhythm. I pulled my right arm…boom…the oars hit the water. Then my left…boom…twenty paddles pulled the boat forward. Everyone chanted "Go…Nick…Go" in time with the drummer and my arm movements.

As we got closer to Burlington, the sheriff boat's siren announced our imminent arrival. A thousand people gathered in a large park on the banks of the Mississippi for Iowa's largest happy hour, the "Port of Burlington Friday Fest." One Friday each month, they celebrated (I never found out exactly what else they celebrated). On this day, they celebrated my Swim. People came to welcome us to their town.

Pat was the first to greet us.

Because of Pat, his wife Mary Anne, and their friends, our time in Burlington was like Christmas. Everywhere we went in this town of 25,000, people knew about us and our cause. The scrolling marquee on the West Burlington Bank read, "Burlington Welcomes Nick Irons, Swimming the Mississippi for MS." Inside, a table was set up selling T-shirts. Similar signs and tables were displayed in grocery stores, pharmacies, and Pat's business, Omni Photography. An auction was held at Westland Mall conducted by Sam, Pat's best friend.

After forty-eight hours, I didn't want to leave this city that felt like home. Pat had become part of the River's history, and Burlington became one of our biggest supporters, raising more money than many other larger cities on the River. Pat's passion and kindness enriched us all.

**Allow people to do what they love.** *Who isn't more productive when they're excited about their job? Put your dream team together and give people an opportunity to do what they're good at and love. Tap into the talents of others and let your dream flourish.*

Andres Benach, a friend and fellow Boston College swimmer, greets his friends with a bear hug and a slap on the back. Everyone likes him. He's smart and loves a good argument. He'll argue about anything. I'd argue that that's why he became a lawyer.

On July 25, at 11:30 p.m., the plane carrying Andres and his girlfriend, Mona, touched down. The captain announced over the loudspeaker, "Welcome to St. Louis. The temperature is currently ninety-two degrees." The heat was the least of Andres' concerns. Nervous and excited, he had flown from Washington, D.C., the day before his twenty-fifth birthday.

A month before the Swim, during a chance encounter with my parents at the Java House (my parents' favorite Washington, D.C., hangout), Andres had heard about my plans. Wanting to help, he became a fundraising machine, selling hundreds of T-shirts to his family, friends, and fellow students at The George Washington University Law School. Complete strangers crossing Andres' path couldn't avoid his convincing pitch. Soon, my parents spotted our green-and-white MS4MS logo everywhere in D.C. But he wasn't satisfied just selling T-shirts; he wanted to "go the extra mile."

Andres and I stood on the back of Dave's boat, just north of St. Louis. I watched him grab his goggles with an I'm-having-second-thoughts look on his face. I didn't blame him. There is something foreboding about staring into the water of the Mississippi, knowing you're about to throw your body into the brown slime.

I jumped in, turned around, and waved at him.

"Come on, get in!" I yelled. "You flew 1,500 miles to do this."

With a bit of hesitation, Andres took the plunge. For six miles, I swam with a friend, stopping occasionally to talk, laugh, and joke. We sprinted, did some butterfly, staged impromptu races to Andy's boat, and had a great time.

Andres was doing what he loved and getting me down the River. Swimming with him changed my mood. Our time together in the water reminded me how much I loved swimming. It also showed me that when I didn't focus on the pain, frustration, and boredom, the time passed a lot faster. "Get me off this River" was no longer my mantra.

**Celebrate along the way.** *Stop often and celebrate your accomplishments with your team. Boost morale, yours and theirs. These happy moments offer an opportunity to reflect on what you've already accomplished.*

Andres and I climbed out of the water, changed into dry clothes, and joined Mona and Andy on the deck of the boat. Dave steered the *Misty Blue* toward my last lock. I had been looking forward to this moment for months. As we waited for the doors of the lock to open, I popped the cork on the bottle of Veuve Clicquot champagne — Andres' contribution to the celebration. As we raised our plastic glasses with the French bubbly, the cell phone rang.

"Hello."

"Nick, it's us." It was my mom, giddy with excitement. "We're flying over the Mississippi River right now. Where are you? We're really close to the water and we're looking for your boat."

My mom and dad were calling from the airplane telephone to our cell phone on their descent into St. Louis, where they were meeting us for the half-way-point celebration. The call came from out of the blue — literally. I had no idea what time they were due to arrive, and they had no idea we were still on the water. But, as they flew over us, my mom felt an irresistible urge to place this outrageously expensive call.

"We're celebrating Andres' birthday and my last lock. We were just about to make a toast with champagne," I said.

"Are you serious? Right now? Congratulations! Have a glass for us."

We raised our glasses and toasted. The song "How Bizarre" by OMC blasted in the background.

## MAKE IT HAPPEN

### LESSON #8: *Put Together a Great Team*

Even if you're the only one in the water, enthusiastic supporters can help you fulfill your dream. Complete the following activities to help you put together your "dream team."

1. Read over your plan and answer the following questions:
   - *In what areas is help a necessity?*
   - *What tasks would be easier with the support of others?*
   - *What tasks don't I want to do?*
   - *What tasks don't I know how to do?*
   - *What tasks don't I have time to do?*

2. Write down the names of at least three people who you would like to be on your team. If you are having trouble, ask yourself:
   - *In my written dream, who was surrounding me?*
   - *Who would be as passionate about my dream as I am?*
   - *Who has the knowledge and skills I need to be successful?*
   - *Whom do I laugh and have fun with?*
   - *Whose strengths complement my weaknesses?*
   - *Whom do I want to celebrate with?*

3. Ask potential team members for their help and share your excitement with them. Write a letter, send an email, pick up the phone, or invite them to dinner.
   - *Ask some people to become permanent members of your team.*
   - *Ask others to complete a specific task.*
   - *Invite people to do what they love.*

*Blessed are the flexible, for they shall not be bent out of shape.*

UNKNOWN

# 9

# GO WITH THE FLOW
## *Be Flexible*

*Every dream is filled with the unknown. In uncharted waters, flexibility moves you over, around, or through any obstacle with ease. You can make a split-second decision or find the perfect solution and never look back. Even when you don't know what's around the next bend, going with the flow will ease you toward your destination.*

~

By the time we arrived in St. Louis, the volume of the dire warnings we had heard daily since leaving Minneapolis increased several notches.

"The River is dangerous...Currents are unpredictable...There's too much pollution...Undertows will suck you under and never let you up...Logs will block your path...Wakes from quarter-mile-long barges will pull you into their engines...The man-eating catfish will swallow you whole."

Armed with little trustworthy information, we entered the unknown waters of the Lower River to face whatever lay ahead. Our lives were about to change.

Towns that had been only a few miles apart on the Upper River were now few and far between. We left St. Louis and traded a world of cable TV, air conditioning, motels, restaurants, and people for life on the *Misty Blue*. For up to five days at a time, we lived on the water — and for Andy and me the change was dramatic. Getting used to our new life proved to be a bigger challenge than "the man-eating catfish" or anything anyone on the Upper River had warned us about.

Anchored in the backwaters of the Mississippi, we learned to make home-cooked meals, sleep in tiny beds, and survive each long day that blurred into the next.

I woke up around 7:30 each morning to the swishing sound of Dave wiping the dew from the deck of the boat. In the still of the early morning, I lay in bed, my thoughts drifting aimlessly. Sometimes I planned my day or fantasized about finishing the Swim; usually I just listened to the quiet splashes of the morning River against the boat and tried to distinguish the chirps of birds nesting on shore.

After my 8:15 a.m. call to Joe and Barbara at WRC and a check-in with my parents, I ate three bowls of Frosted Flakes with a mango on the side, chatted with Dave, and watched the blue herons perched on rocks nearby. The statuesque birds, so close I could see their eyes, stood completely still, staring into the water until they found their perfect meal. In the blink of an eye, even before we knew what was happening, they pounced, catching their prey with powerful beaks.

By 9:00, Andy rolled out of bed, his hair screaming, "Don't say a word, I just woke up." Thirty minutes later, we were in the water as usual, ready for another fifteen-mile day. About 11:00 or 11:30, we climbed back onto the *Misty Blue*, having completed a six- or seven-mile swim. Then lunch — sandwiches (or pasta if Andy decided to cook), a call to my parents to take care of any lingering details, and I was back in bed for a long afternoon nap. Sleep eased the constant ache of my sore muscles and gave me refuge from the ever-present heat.

While I slept, Dave retreated to the bridge to watch the barges move their giant loads of cargo up and down the River. Intrigued by these monsters of commerce, he wrote their names in his journal next to stories he wanted to bring back to his wife, Judy.

Andy puttered to shore for some alone time to relax and work on a piece of art he titled "Master Plan." His canvas — his eight-horsepower motor. His medium — crayons of all colors melted in the sun. In late afternoon, I jumped into the water to finish the miles for the day. These later swims, when the weather was ten degrees cooler and the River calmer, became Andy's favorite time. He watched carp jump and swallows circle around us.

Each night after my last swim, I grabbed a bottle of shampoo, stood on the back of the boat, and "showered," scrubbing slime off my hair and body before rinsing with a gallon of warm water that had been heating all day in the sun. Then time for dinner.

With an abundance of free time on our hands, we ate well. We grilled chicken and steaks, and cooked pasta and rice. Actually, *Andy* grilled chicken and steaks, and *Andy* cooked pasta and rice. My four specialties — rum cake, tuna dip, Caesar salad, and baked potatoes — never made it onto the menu aboard the *Misty Blue*. Andy mastered cooking in the boat's two- by three-foot kitchen. Dave and I did the dishes.

After dinner, we searched the airwaves to find music on the FM radio. Sometimes we were lucky and found a far-off radio station. If that didn't work, we resorted to Dave's tape collection to play his best tapes — Neil Diamond and Willie Nelson. Andy settled inside the cabin, hidden from the mosquitoes and mayflies that loved munching on his body. He wrote into the early morning hours, while Dave and I fell asleep by nine o'clock. Cross off another day.

We eased into our new life — learning to deal with the barge traffic that chilled people on the Upper River and kept pleasure boaters off the Lower Mississippi, and the monotony of endless hours on the water.

Now, masters of flexibility, we welcomed any change in our daily routine.

About four o'clock one afternoon, I pulled my prescription goggles onto my face and jumped into the water to swim hours five and six for the day. Still a bit groggy after my two-hour nap, I glanced upward. Clouds moved in all directions, and blackness darkened the sky behind us. A quiet stillness made the splash of my stroke sound like the crash of an ocean wave. An eerie glow sat just above the water.

The impending thunderstorm brought me back to the Great Plains and my childhood in Oklahoma. As a kid, my love of violent storms would lure me outdoors to watch the energy build-up as clouds looming on the horizon inched their way toward me. I loved seeing flashes of lightning and a curtain of rain in the distance, and the smell of an imminent storm.

For nearly an hour, I watched, captivated by the storm slowly chasing me down — closer, closer, closer. I rolled onto my back to get a better look when Dave yelled to Andy, his tone laced with fear, "GET 'M OUT!"

The lure of the storm had me in its grip. I was loving swimming. Andy knew that if we stopped early, it would throw us off schedule. Our already long days would be even longer if we had to make up the distance. With only three miles to go, neither of us wanted to stop. Dave wanted no part of it. My swim for the day was definitely over.

Andy and I headed for his boat and climbed aboard.

"This is a big one. They just reported a tornado touch-down three miles back — right where we ate lunch." Dave's voice trembled.

He piloted the boat downstream to search for a safe place to anchor for the night. We scoured the shoreline for a protected cove, far away from the channel and barges. We looked for safety from the logs, tree branches, and debris that would soon flow into the River.

"How about over there?" I asked, pointing to a secluded section of the River.

Dave steered into the cove, our home for the night, and stopped the engine. We raced against nature. Sheets of rain in the distance were no longer inching slowly, but speeding toward us. All three of us sprung into action. Everyone knew what to do.

We threw the first anchor in front of the bow. With a bit of luck, it caught immediately. We secured two more anchors to the back. The boat wasn't going anywhere.

Andy prepared his dinghy by clearing out a radio, life jackets, seat cushions, paddles, and other miscellaneous paraphernalia, before tying it a bit more securely to the *Misty Blue*. I ran through the main cabin and closed all ten windows. When I finished, I climbed to the bridge and grabbed the two metal and fiberglass antennas that rose thirty feet into the air and flanked either side of the boat. I saw a bolt of lightning in the distance. What was I doing? Why not just paint a bull's-eye on my back? I took those antennas down faster than they had ever come down before.

In a mere five minutes, we were ready for whatever the storm had in store for us. We each took one last walk around the boat, and made sure everything was secure. We snapped a few pictures and retreated inside.

Dave scanned the stations of his marine radio. The news gave us more reason to worry. Towboats — marvels in technology, equipped with the latest electronics, satellite navigation, and radar to see weather patterns for hundreds of miles — had decided to anchor their load. These giants that travel twenty-four hours a day through rain, hail, wind, and snow were waiting out the storm on the side of the River — an ominous sign. This night, even the tow captains worried.

Rain, propelled by the wind, pelted down on us while waves crashed against the bow, making a deafening roar inside the cabin.

The peaceful rocking that had become a part of our waking lives became violent. Our five-gallon jug of water flew off the counter as if it were weightless.

All night long, the storm pounded the *Misty Blue*. Wind thrust the boat back and forth. In the morning, exhausted from a sleepless night of rocking and worry, we emerged from the cabin. Logs the size of small trees bobbed in the water now dark brown with the mud stirred from the bottom. Twigs, sticks, branches, and everything else that had littered the shore floated in the swift current. Andy's dinghy was filled with muddy goo.

The excitement of the last twelve hours now behind us, we started all over again.

# LESSON #9
## *Be Flexible*

Going with the flow makes your journey easier — no matter what obstacles you face. Even when calm days give way to gusts of wind and rain, with flexibility, you'll weather any storm.

When you let yourself go with the flow and are willing to make changes as you learn, you'll find that you worry less and enjoy the process of completing your goals more. Use flexibility to take a break from your dream so you can continue with your spirit renewed.

**Go with the flow.** *In pursuit of your dream, problems will arise. Don't stress. Relax. Trust that the current will take you to your destination. Unexpected moments, handled with grace, are often the ones you'll remember for a lifetime.*

Ever since I can remember, flexibility has allowed me to find answers to problems. Although the solutions often seem unconventional to other people, they make perfect sense to me.

In fifth grade, I joined a band. I'm not talking about a jazz band, or a rock band. I joined a marching band, but we never made it to the marching part.

When I entered the band room on the first day, my eyes grew huge. There before me stood a room full of shiny instruments. I saw drums and trumpets, a sax or two, clarinets and flutes, a piccolo — so many choices. Which should I choose?

I walked slowly down the line of instruments. I picked each one up to see how it felt. The flute looked funny in my big hands. The sax felt better but looked so goofy, and there, between the trumpet and clarinet, the baritone called my name.

I had never seen this wonderful instrument before. It looked just like a tuba — only smaller. It was heavy like a tuba and when I blew into the mouthpiece the billowing tuba noises made me laugh. I liked it. Big and different from all the others, it fit my personality.

For the next four months, it was my instrument. Twice a week, I proudly lugged this monstrosity to and from band practice. Those spoiled piccolo players had it so easy.

Every practice we prepared for our moment at the closing recital. We worked hard for those three minutes. When the exciting day came we dressed up in our best clothes — ties included — and took our places on the high school stage.

We sat, forty ten-year-olds, on chairs in the middle of what I imagined Carnegie Hall must be like. I adjusted the sheet music, picked up the baritone, and could barely wait for the conductor to give the cue to make music. Her hand fell; I began to play.

I played and played and played. The notes flowed out of my instrument, as I had never heard before. I was on fire. I played...turned the page...played...turned the page...until I reached the end. I pulled the baritone away from my mouth and took a deep breath expecting to hear wild applause and a roar from the crowd.

Instead, the sounds I heard came from the rest of my band — still playing. They were only half-way through the piece. I had played so fast that I had left them in my dust.

What do I do now? I couldn't just sit there waiting for everyone to finish.

So I started over. I played...and played...and played some more, until everyone finally caught up with me and finished the piece.

**Change your direction as you learn.** *While you complete your dream, you will gain knowledge and build skills. New insights can improve even the best-thought-out plans. Don't hesitate to use this new information to choose a different path, find a new way, or figure out a solution.*

The lower half of the Mississippi is ruled by commerce. At least once an hour, we passed enormous barge chains five acres in size. Huge towboats pushed as many as forty-nine flatbed barges, sitting side by side, seven wide by seven deep — much larger than the largest load we had passed on the Upper River (fifteen flatbeds, three wide by five deep). Nine-thousand-horsepower engines filled the air with a devilish whine similar to that of a fighter jet.

One complete barge chain could carry the equivalent of 2,800 semi-trailer loads, or enough wheat to bake 110 *million* loaves of bread. The turbulence from the barges could be dangerous, producing waves up to seven feet high.

When I began my Swim in Minnesota, we heard dire words of warning: "Get too close to the barges and they will suck you under."

At first, we believed the hype and were terrified. Whenever a barge approached, I hopped into Andy's boat and waited five or ten minutes until it passed. Swimming became tedious and our days longer.

As we gained first-hand information about the River traffic on the Lower Mississippi, Andy and Dave began thinking like the barge captains. They understood where the barges wanted to go and steered me to the opposite side of the channel. I never stopped swimming to let them pass again.

**Open yourself to adventure.** *By being flexible, you allow yourself to experience everything life has to offer. You'll meet new people, see new things, and have a great time. Every new experience adds flavor to your dream.*

The day before our arrival in Natchez, Mississippi, my dad randomly called the manager at "The Burn," a beautiful antebellum bed and breakfast listed on the National Register of Historic Places.

Layne was taken aback by the call. After seeing our story the night before on a TV newscast from Jackson, Mississippi (over a hundred miles away), he dreamt that we had stayed in his B&B. Viewing my dad's call as an obvious omen, he excitedly called the owners of the Inn. With their blessing, he offered us rooms. He then took it upon himself to make sure we enjoyed our stay in Natchez.

We had planned to relax in the luxury of this spectacular inn and lounge by the pool all day. Instead we changed our plans, trusting Layne to guide us.

Our day off started with a tour of Monmouth Plantation, a classic Southern mansion straight out of *Gone With the Wind*. I expected to bump into Scarlett and Rhett standing in the doorway.

For lunch, we went to a second plantation, Stanton Hall, to eat Southern cooking at its best. As we sipped sweetened tea, surrounded by Natchez's rich and famous, Layne offered us two choices.

"Okay, guys. This afternoon you can either visit Longwood Plantation, the largest octagonal house in the country, like I had originally planned, or enjoy some 'Knock-You-Naked' margaritas."

Let's just say, it was an easy decision. The rest of the afternoon was not spent in a house shaped like a stop sign, but instead on the deck of a log cabin called "Fat Mama's," under the shade of poplar trees, enjoying the best margaritas north of the Rio Grande.

**Take a break from your dream.** *When you're working on your dream, it's easy to become consumed by it. Burnout often comes next. Let yourself take a break without a plan for an hour, a day, or a week. You can calm your mind, fill a void, or learn something new. You'll return to your dream with renewed spirit.*

Steve Skarky, a high school friend of mine, had agreed to work for the *Mississippi Swim* for two months on the Upper River. He handled on-land logistics and also drove a rental car, our transportation when we were out of the water.

In a small town, we drove from the River to our motel, passing a windowless bar. A prominent banner hung outside: "Tyson Fight Airing Tonight." Since we had nothing better to do that evening, the idea of watching Mike Tyson seemed inviting — who knew what bizarreness we might witness.

Steve stopped the car and went in to check the time of the fight, while Andy and I sat patiently. We waited…and waited…and waited.

"Maybe he's just getting us free food," I thought aloud, as I relaxed into the seat.

After fifteen minutes, we began to worry. As we were about to go in to see if he was all right, he bounced out grinning.

"What's so funny?" I asked.

"We've been invited to a wedding reception," he announced.

"Are we going?" I laughed.

When Steve entered the place, he had found a tuxedo-clad owner behind the bar. They struck up a conversation, and Steve discovered that he not only knew my story, but he had been following me since I left Minnesota.

He had just come from his daughter's wedding and had stopped by the bar to pick up some cases of beer. He would be honored if we joined him, as his guests, for the reception.

How could we pass up an opportunity like that?

We drove to the hotel to shower and change into the dressiest khaki pants and MS4MS shirts we had. We returned to meet the new father-in-law a couple of hours later, under a large tent in his backyard. He proudly introduced us to everyone — the bride and groom, friends, and guests. I reached out to shake hands with his wife as she shot her husband a look-of-death that said, "Who are these strangers and why are they here and you had better have a good explanation."

With that, our host excused himself and followed his wife to the head table to join the wedding party. We spent the rest of the evening celebrating the glorious occasion in small-town America, listening to speeches by the best man and maid of honor, and toasting the happy couple. By the end of the evening, even the mother of the bride forgot we were strangers. Toasts and laughs fueled me for another week.

## MAKE IT HAPPEN

### LESSON #9: *Be Flexible*

Let yourself be flexible. Relax. Don't stress; everything will work out fine. If that's difficult for you, these activities will help you go with the flow.

1. Give up your need for control.
   Suggestions:
   - *Go whitewater rafting.*
   - *Fly in an airplane.*
   - *Let your spouse drive.*
   - *Leave your watch at home.*
   - *Let people working for you run a meeting.*

2. Think of a time when you changed your plan because you learned something new.
   - *Where were you?*
   - *Would your plan have worked without making the change?*
   - *Would your plan have worked as well without the change?*
   - *Are you glad you made the change?*

3. Take a break from your routine at least once in the next week.
   Suggestions:
   - *Get in the car and drive with no destination in mind.*
   - *Take a walk — let your body tell you where to go.*
   - *Go shopping. Try on those leather pants you would never, ever, ever buy.*

Jumping off the *Misty Blue*

A moment off for Dave

Memphis, here we come!

A mighty tow boat

A large barge

Jessica and Judy bringing a touch of home

Still having fun

One brilliant sunset

Our "clean boat"

A clean me

Storm clouds on the horizon

Andy's home for four months

A conversation worth noting

Mr. Mayor

*Imagination is more important
than knowledge.*

ALBERT EINSTEIN

# 10

# THAT'S RANDOM!
## Be Creative

*From beginning to end, creativity is at the core of every dream.*
*Creativity brings an idea to life and keeps it breathing.*
*With creativity, good times become great times, and*
*problems have solutions. Anything is possible.*
~

It was late August and Dave tuned his radio to the weather channel. "We have oppressive heat in store for us. We'll see 100-degree days with eighty-degree nights for the entire week."

After three months of battling the elements, none of us were in the mood for "oppressive" anything. We left the heat aboard the *Misty Blue* to find an oasis in Memphis, Tennessee.

Making our way through the heartland of America, we met many people who enriched our adventure and helped us taste the flavor of each new area. Sometimes we ran into them in little diners on "Main Street" in towns with one stoplight, just like in my pre-Swim fantasy. Sometimes, in a grocery store over the meat counter. Walking into a room wearing our official MS4MS T-shirts was enough to stop conversations in mid-sentence and invite questions from townspeople who had heard about "the man swimming the Mississippi."

By the time we made our way to Memphis, Andy and I longed for anonymity. All we wanted to do was relax, act like typical twenty-somethings, and forget we represented a cause. In Memphis, we could blend in with the other tourists. We joined the crowd at Graceland, where the green shag-carpeted walls, mirrored ceilings, and Elvis' favorite monkey statues helped us feel as far away from the Mississippi as possible.

Judy, Dave's wife of thirty-seven years, flew in from Cedar Rapids, and Jessica, the love of Andy's life, traveled for thirty-six hours by train from New York City to meet us. For three days of fun, my faithful companions smiled broad grins that raised their spirits — and mine. We did taste-tests comparing "wet" and "dry" Memphis barbeque, hung out on Beale Street, and sang the blues.

Living as we had for the past three months, isolated in the middle of the River, we lost all sense of reality. In Memphis, we lived a "normal" life again. Judy and Jessica brought with them love and a touch of the outside world and home. They reminded me that there were other people out there, to whom we weren't strangers, who knew and cared about us.

As quickly as it came, our sabbatical ended. Dave and Andy said tearful goodbyes — Dave at the airport and Andy at the train station. *Misty Blue* couldn't have been a more appropriate name for Dave's boat as we climbed aboard in mournful silence. We all knew we had thirty-six days and 500 miles ahead of us. It seemed as if our journey was just beginning.

Back on the water, we found our "friend," oppressive heat, right where we had left it, partying on our boat. None of us laughed a lot that day. Although the *Misty Blue* served as a wonderfully comfortable refuge, let's face it, it was still a boat. The next town on the River was seventy-five miles downstream. We knew we would be spending five days living in a small, one-bedroom space with no air-conditioning while temperatures hovered between eighty and 100 degrees day and night.

But, we all knew we had a job to complete, and we fell back into our routine. I swam, my shoulder aching a bit more than usual. Andy tried to keep his sanity by singing Christmas carols as he puttered at four miles per hour in his tiny inflatable for hours in the blistering sun. Dave followed behind, protecting us from the three-block-long barges that were now a part of our daily life on the Lower Mississippi.

To while away the time, Dave talked by radio to the tow captains maneuvering their barges up and down the River. Many of the captains knew about the Swim and chatted with him — a fun diversion for Dave. He also learned more about the River he had always wanted to navigate.

On the morning of our third day on the water, Dave placed a call to all tow captains within radio range: "The *Mississippi Swim for Multiple Sclerosis* is thirty miles south of Memphis."

One answered, "How far's he goin' today?"

"He's got another twelve miles," Dave replied.

"Where you stoppin' for the night?"

Dave studied his worn navigational chart of the Mississippi for an answer and replied, "I think we'll stop around Buck Island Light."

"Well, good luck tonight at the casinos."

"Thanks," Dave said, completely confused by the conversation. Casinos? What casinos? There were no casinos nearby on his 1994 chart. There weren't even *towns* on his chart.

With the three of us back on the boat taking a break after the first two hours of swimming, Dave mentioned his conversation with the tow captain.

"Are you serious?" Andy and I asked in unison as we bounded around the bridge like a couple of crazed lunatics.

"A hotel. There has to be a hotel. Where there are casinos,

there are hotels."

I grabbed the phone, praying this fantasy was somehow real, and called our support team in Washington.

"Hi, Mom." I tried to sound calm. "Do you think you or Dad could find hotel rooms for us for tonight? We heard there are casinos somewhere in the area. We're just south of Memphis."

"Let me work on it."

My mom's title, "PR Goddess," was about to be put to the ultimate test. I knew if anybody could make this work, she could.

Less than an hour later, the phone rang. "The rumors are true." My heart skipped a beat when I heard my mom's magical words.

"You'll be stopping a half-mile from Tunica, Mississippi. The Horseshoe is waiting for you with open arms."

She casually mentioned that there was one "slight problem" — a field of gangly weeds separated Tunica from the water. There was no road between the town and the River and no way for us to get to the hotel.

"But don't worry," she reassured me. "They're working on it." Whatever that meant.

Buoyed by trust and hope, I kept swimming.

As we approached a secluded cove, flashing yellow lights atop a white SUV caught my attention. A half-dozen grinning employees from the Horseshoe lined the shore clapping and cheering. Behind the smiling faces, I saw their creative solution to our problem.

There before us was a road. A new road. *Our* road. Using a bulldozer and backhoe, the hotel's maintenance department had spent the afternoon cutting through the field to shape a passage. Now they stood like artists displaying their work.

Dave and Andy secured their boats and we waded out of the muddy water. We were met with handshakes, smiles, and pats on the back.

"Welcome to Tunica."

"Welcome to the Horseshoe."

Swiftly we were ushered away by SUV. Caught in a maze of plants we drove farther and farther on our new road. It started to feel as if I was stuck in a bizarre dream. Were these people real? Where were they taking us? Before my imagination could spiral out of control, we entered a clearing. I gazed at the multicolored city that blinked on and off before me. A half-dozen high-rise buildings glowing in neon — like Las Vegas and then some. In front of us, in all its grandeur, stood the Horseshoe Casino.

Our hosts whisked us off to the gift shop to replace our muddy clothing with anything we wanted, then brought us to our luxurious suite, the size of five boats, which included large, cushy beds, and heavenly, bone-chillingly-cold air conditioning.

After some time to shower and relax, we met the staff gathered in the lobby outside Jack Binion's Steakhouse for a "special presentation." Several guests joined us, watching as the casino host showered us with warm words of appreciation for our efforts.

In a day filled with surprises, he presented us with another one — a giant cardboard check reading, "Pay to the order of: *The Mississippi Swim for Multiple Sclerosis.*" We accepted a cashable check for $1,000, the Horseshoe's donation to MS research.

# LESSON #10
## *Be Creative*

Creativity is the very essence of a successful dream. Whether it's discovering a compelling idea, devising a plan, or making it happen, it's impossible to complete a dream without it.

Discover the many aspects of your creativity by noticing the innovative or resourceful moments in your life. Think in new ways. Look for opportunities to use ingenuity to enhance your dream.

Creative ideas are only as limited as your imagination. Unleash your creativity and your dream will surpass your wildest expectations.

**Think of yourself as creative.** *Everyone is creative. You use creativity to deal with finances, to plan a menu, or to raise a family. You can crunch numbers, wait tables, or make deliveries creatively. Notice the innovative ways you handle the ordinary moments of your life and you'll discover what makes you creative.*

To manage our lives on the Swim, we had to be creative — every day. We learned to handle swimming and safety concerns on the water. Off the water, we needed food, shelter (for a boat as well as for us), supplies, and transportation. With little to no money, our resourcefulness abounded. There were reporters to deal with, and our sanity was always at stake. Whatever was necessary, we had to find it — one way or another.

Finding safe places to dock the *Misty Blue*, while we stayed on shore, became a pressing concern. Marinas, like those on the Upper Mississippi, were few and far between once we got past St. Louis. In two months, we attached the boat alongside a Coast Guard cutter, tied it to a casino boat, docked it in a barge repair shop, hooked it onto a ferry station, and parked it in a cove under the watchful eye of a security guard.

Once our boat was safely docked, we walked to the nearest parking lot. It usually took a bit of ingenuity to find a ride to our hotel. We hitched rides with hotel and motel owners, two newspaper editors, a television production crew, two mayors, one dockworker, a few security people, and a bartender. We rode in the front and the back of a pickup truck and in vehicles with and without sirens.

Because we traveled light, every day we had to restock our supplies. We found generous supporters who gave us groceries, gas, and boating supplies. People often threw in extra treasures — books about the Mississippi, commemorative T-shirts and hats, a radio, candy or cookies, and Dave's favorite, six-dozen homemade tamales.

We went on a daily crusade to find free food, which led us to meals in people's homes, local diners, all-you-can-eat buffets, fast-food chains, and an occasional five-star restaurant.

For over four months I gave interviews — in person or by cell phone. I spoke with reporters while standing on the banks of the River, on a sandy beach, on docks and piers, in marinas, on the *Mississippi Queen*, under the St. Louis Arch, and just outside Graceland. I talked by phone while lounging on the back of the boat, lying in bed, sitting in a car, restaurant or bar, standing on top of an SUV, or hanging onto Andy's boat while still in the water.

We found entertainment by talking ourselves into free tickets to an Air Supply concert, a "Men's Review," a boxing match, and two minor-league baseball games. The Blues Festival and wedding found us.

On our days off, we learned fun facts about the Mississippi and the people who lived along it. We were given guided tours of Trempealeau, Wisconsin; Burlington, Iowa; plantations in Mississippi and Arkansas; and the bayous of Louisiana. We learned about the Great Flood of 1993, the history of the lock and dam system, the best bullet to use when hunting armadillo, and how to measure an alligator by looking at the length of its nose. We attended a city council meeting, MS support groups, and kids' swim team practices, and were given official proclamations by several mayors, as well as the key to two cities.

We used our creativity and came away with a scrapbook of memories to last a lifetime.

**Think in new ways.** *There's always more than one way to solve a problem, overcome an obstacle, or make a task easier. Sometimes, it helps to break the rules. Look at all options and then try new ideas. Be creative and you'll find novel ways to accomplish your dream. You don't have to fly or take a train to reach your destination; cross-country skiing may be a better way to go.*

In response to one of my dad's random phone calls, David Lush, a reporter from Rosedale, Mississippi, offered us food, friendship and his home for the night. We shared a delicious dinner with David and his wife and a few of their friends, including the mayor of Rosedale.

As we twirled our spaghetti, we got to know J.Y. Trice (or as he prefers, "Mr. Mayor"), a distinguished man who looked younger than his seventy-some years. He had begun his life in politics as a hobby, as a way of continuing to make a difference in this world after he retired as the local high school principal.

I got a kick out of his "rule-breaking" approach to life.

He had decided not to let his dislike for political campaigning keep him from doing what he loved — serving the people. After his first election, he influenced the city council to change the law affecting the mayoral term. He wouldn't have to run every two years; it was now a four-year stint.

Mr. Mayor commanded the power and respect of the area. Politically he was a force to reckon with, not only in Rosedale but in the entire state of Mississippi.

In November of an election year, townspeople called his office to ask his advice. Whom should they vote for? He held the votes of his loyal supporters in his hands. His influence did a lot to help this area rife with poverty.

State and federal congressmen were well aware of his prestige with voters, so they tried to keep him happy by designating state and federal money to help build commercial projects, parks and schools in Rosedale.

While we were in town, the mayor took care of us personally, arranging transportation and making sure we were well-fed and happy. Before we left, he brought us to the local Piggly Wiggly grocery store to pick up supplies.

As we wandered from aisle to aisle, I heard a respectful tone, "Hello, Mr. Mayor."

"How are you, Joe? How's Betty?"

I witnessed him in action. Every conversation ended with the words, "If there is anything I can do for you, just let me know." Judging from the care he showed us, complete strangers, he meant it.

After talking with everyone in the store, he helped us shop. I'll never forget Andy asking, "Mr. Mayor, could you hand me some peas?"

When I mentioned to our new friend that I was going to be on *Good Morning America* when I finished my Swim in September, he said, "Well, that's all right!"

He promised to tell everyone in town about it. Was he going to put it in the newspaper? "No, not everyone reads the newspaper." Was he going to tell people during his weekly radio address? "No, not everyone listens to the radio." Was he going to bring it up at the next city council meeting? "No, not everyone attends." As mayor, he had devised an unconventional way to communicate with his supporters. "I'll put a notice in next month's water bill. Everyone reads their water bill."

**Let yourself see creative opportunities.** *There is a better way to do almost everything. Be open to seeing creative ideas — yours or someone else's — that enhance your dream. You may discover something you never realized you needed, and then wonder how you ever did without it. Stand back and look at your dream. How are you accomplishing it? Is there a better way? What can you (or someone else) do to make your journey easier, safer, or more fun?*

I expected it to be hot during the Swim. Andy and I had grown up in Oklahoma, so we knew what heat was. During the summer between my third and fourth grades, temperatures soared over 100 degrees for fifty days in a row.

The weather along the Mississippi River in the summer of 1997 was hotter than I'd expected. There was little rain and the temperatures climbed. Eight hours a day in the blazing sun tanned our bodies to the darkest Coppertone shade. We drank gallons of Gatorade, but the sweltering conditions still drained every ounce of our energy.

Anxious to experience the Swim up close and personal, Bob and Marca Floyd and Jimmy and Debby Goodman, four of my parents' best friends and a constant part of my childhood, found us in the middle of the River two days north of St. Louis. Arriving from Oklahoma City to join our celebration in St. Louis, they started the weekend by spending two hours on the bridge of the *Misty Blue* with Dave as we made our way toward Alton, Illinois.

They laughed and cheered me on and were having a great time. After an hour of burning sun, even these lifelong Oklahoma residents started feeling its effects. Both Marca and Debby went into the cabin to escape the soaring temperature and burning rays of the sun.

Bob and Jimmy dripped with sweat, but they stayed on top with Dave.

We stopped in Alton to grab some Cokes in the air-conditioned comfort of the marina. Several times, I noticed a whispering Bob and Jimmy duo. I turned to say something to Andy, and when I looked back they had vanished. A few minutes later, Dave noticed them crawling around the bridge of the *Misty Blue* with a tape measure. What in the world were they doing?

Soon they were back in the marina, pen and paper in hand, making phone calls. By the time we left Alton, a new canvas Bimini Top had been ordered for Dave's boat. It would be shipped to us in Cape Girardeau.

The beautiful royal blue sun-shield that would protect Dave from blistering rays was neatly installed a week later, ready to keep us safe and sane for the remaining two-and-a-half months of our journey.

Thanks to the creativity, kindness and generosity of the Floyds and Goodmans, Dave stood on the bridge all day in the shade, protected from the fiery sun. The rays no longer beat down directly on the boat, so even the temperature inside was lower. We spent many days under the fine-looking blue cover, remembering the friends who took it upon themselves to make our journey a little easier.

## MAKE IT HAPPEN

### LESSON #10: *Be Creative*

Discover the creativity you already have and build upon it. Complete the following activities to sharpen your creative skills.

1. Think of a time in your life when others could have called you "Mr. or Ms. Creative."
   - *How would you have earned this title?*
   - *What came from your use of creativity?*
2. Think of a problem you're facing, at home or at the office. Look "outside the box" for the answer.
   - *How can you attack the problem differently?*
   - *What haven't you tried?*
   - *What is the most unconventional answer to this problem?*
   - *What rules do you need to break to solve this problem?*
   - *How would an eight-year-old solve this problem?*

3. Get together with the most creative people you know. Ask them questions to find out:
    - *How they became so creative.*
    - *How they stay creative.*
    - *When they're most creative.*
    - *Where their creative ideas come from.*

# A Dream Come True

At last… Baton Rouge

Together with my family…the end of a long journey

*Life's like a movie*
*Write your own ending*
*Keep believing*
*Keep pretending*
*We've done just what we set out to do*

"THE MAGIC STORE"
KERMIT THE FROG
WRITTEN BY PAUL WILLIAMS
& KENNETH ASCHER

# 11

# RAISE A GLASS

On September 25, 1997, the day before my dad's fifty-third birthday, Andy, Dave, and I sat on the bridge of the *Misty Blue*, anchored five miles north of the 12th Street Bridge in Baton Rouge, Louisiana. Five miles from our finish line. Five miles from my family.

The atmosphere on the boat was electric. Andy would soon be seeing Jessica and starting his career in New York City. Dave would meet Judy in Baton Rouge and the two would travel the River to New Orleans before heading home by plane to Iowa. (The *Misty Blue* would return on the back of a truck.)

I felt lighter than I had in months, and it wasn't just my forty-pound weight loss. The burdens weighing on my shoulders had been lifted. After two years of stressing, planning, interviewing, fundraising, and swimming, I was five miles from my dream and giddy with excitement.

"Do you think Domino's will deliver out here?" I yelled. Andy laughed.

Instead, we cooked all the leftover food on the boat. Looking into the kitchen, you would have thought we were catering a gourmet dinner for fifty. Water boiled for pasta, chicken marinated in olive oil, garlic and oregano, and salad greens were piled high waiting for dressing. We ate like kings.

Dave, Andy, and I savored our long, leisurely dinner on the boat — no reporters, no interruptions, just the three of us together one last time. We reminisced about St. Louis, the Horseshoe, the man-eating catfish stories, long days on the water, and fun times in Memphis. We talked about the Mayor, and the wedding, and all the people who had gone out of their way to make our adventure easier, more fun, memorable, and successful.

Eventually, we passed around the cell phone. I talked with friends in Los Angeles. Dave called his kids and grandkids in Iowa, and Andy spent his time talking to Jessica in New York. With congratulations ringing in our ears, we lay down to sleep.

I didn't get much sleep that night. There were too many thoughts bouncing off the walls of my mind. As I lay in the darkness listening to waves splash against the bow, I thought back to the day I sat at a desk in Los Angeles writing out my treatment. Since then, I had lived the upcoming twenty-four hours in my imagination a thousand times.

Would tomorrow live up to my expectations? I drifted into a fitful sleep.

I rose before the sun, threw on some warm clothes to protect myself from the unseasonably cool weather, and joined Dave on the deck. We sat in silence, watching the sunrise over the Mississippi River. No words were spoken; no words were needed.

Shortly after breakfast, we saw two small boats coming toward us. Brian Spillman and deputies from the Louisiana Department of Wildlife and Fisheries arrived fully prepared to make a scene as they escorted us into Baton Rouge. Their boats were decked out with flashing lights and sirens. This day, with their help, we would control the Mississippi River — even tow captains would yield to us.

Around 10 a.m., three boats filled with media joined our entourage. Before I knew it, reporters and camera people from the

*Baton Rouge Advocate*, the *Minneapolis Star-Tribune*, *People* magazine, and *Good Morning America* descended on the *Misty Blue*. They fired questions at me.

"How does it feel to be finishing?"

"How are you going to feel as you climb on shore?"

"How will you feel when you see your dad for the first time?"

All these *feel* questions had kept me awake the night before. I didn't have any answers, so I pretended to have other things to do. Brushing my teeth worked especially well, because even if I wanted to talk, I couldn't with a toothbrush in my mouth. My teeth were SOOO white by the time I was finished. The reporters followed me around our overcrowded boat until, finally, I closed the cabin door to change.

At exactly 11 a.m., Andy climbed into his inflatable boat for the last time — ever. He pulled the cord, started the engine on our last day, and motored away. I laced up my Speedo, adjusted my goggles, and yelled "woo hoo" as I jumped into the muddy water.

I felt a lump in the back of my throat and fought back tears. This was the last time I would jump off the side of Dave's boat yelling "woo hoo" or look up and see Andy guiding my way. Anticipation of the celebration less than an hour away mixed with sadness that my adventure of a lifetime was about to end. Suddenly, the four months that had seemed to drag on forever were gone in the blink of an eye. I would miss Dave and Andy being in my life everyday…meeting new people…seeing new places…the buzz of excitement when reporters were around…orange and red sunsets…blue herons…working with my family toward a goal that mattered…and laughing with Andy.

The first thirty minutes of the swim were harder than usual. My shoulders ached the dull ache that for the last month had tugged at my determination to finish. For the last three weeks, I had been worrying about doing permanent damage to my rotator cuff. As I raised my left arm to stroke, I heard a loud "POP" and instantly, the pain vanished. It was as if my body was saying, "I'll get you to Baton Rouge, but after that you're on your own." What happened inside my arm is anyone's guess, but somehow, as always, my body found the strength to keep going.

After the pop, I swam faster than I had in months. My arms felt strong, my legs powerful. I was moving. Too fast. At this rate we would arrive fifteen minutes early. As soon as I stopped to take a break, the phone rang. My parents waited for us on shore. They could see our support boats.

"Nick, you can't arrive before noon," my mom said, completing her last PR stint. "The press is expecting you at noon."

"But we're right here." I thought I would burst.

"Just hang out for few minutes," she said.

"Okay. See you soon," I said as I handed the phone to Andy.

Andy and I had a little more time together. The two of us floated in the river, surrounded by six escort boats, cracking jokes with our companions. I savored one last moment with him, feeling lucky to have him as my brother.

Andy checked his watch and asked, "Ready?"

"Let's do it," I said as I let go of his boat, as I had done so many times before.

After one final turn, I saw the crowd waiting on shore. All of a sudden, I heard the noise. The Department of Wildlife and Fisheries boats blasted their sirens. Dave blew his horn and pressed the button on the can of compressed air he had been saving for this very moment; even the press boats joined in and honked their horns. When the crowd on shore heard the noise, they began to roar — yelling, clapping, and whistling.

With thirty powerful strokes, I swam to the end of my journey.

As I climbed on shore, I was overwhelmed with joy…sheer joy. A large permanent smile, bigger than usual, showed each glistening white tooth in my mouth. Nothing could erase it from my face that day.

Nearly a hundred people lined the bank of the River. Members of the Louisiana State University (LSU) marching band played rousing music in the background. The LSU Men's and Women's swim teams shouted and cheered. I saw a kids' swim team and an MS support group with "Thanks, Nick" signs. My Grandfather Irons, Aunt Lynn and Great-Aunt Babe, lifelong friends Jon and Jed Redwine, and my parents' friends Susan and Joe had all flown in from across the country to celebrate.

As I waded out of the muddy water, the media were in a frenzy. Reporters approached me with microphones in hand, barking questions:

"Nick, you just swam 1,550 miles of the Mississippi River to help your dad. How do you feel?"

"How did you stay healthy along the way?"

And my favorite, "Is this your first trip to Baton Rouge?"

This was my opportunity to address the world, but I had no words. Finally, I uttered one sentence...over and over.

"This is great," I said to one reporter

"This is great," I said again.

"This is great."

All I wanted to do was find my family. I pushed my way through the crowd, saw my dad smiling through his tears, reached out and put my arms around him giving him a huge, wet hug.

"Happy Birthday, Dad...I did this for you," I whispered.

Andy joined us soon after he secured his boat. My mom, dad, John, Andy, and I stood as a family shoulder-to-shoulder, arms around each other. The cameras clicked and flashed and gave us a chance to hold onto each other a little longer. It would be the perfect picture to forever remember an unforgettable journey.

After a weekend of celebration, I left my Mississippi adventure. From an airplane flying just above the River, I gazed down at the brown water one last time and watched as it trailed into the distance. My life had come full circle. What had started as a crazy idea 30,000 feet in the air almost two years earlier was now a reality. One last flood of mixed emotion filled my body.

What did we achieve? Millions of people learned something about multiple sclerosis, even if just how to pronounce the name. Almost $100,000 would go to research. I had accomplished an incredible swim and even with all of the struggles, we'd had fun every step of the way.

I wondered if I'd known two years earlier what I knew now, would I have gone through with my plans? In a heartbeat.

So there you have it — my dream, start to finish.

Now, it's your turn. You have all it takes to make your dream come true. Use what you've learned to fashion your compelling idea into an amazing dream, and before you know it, you'll be climbing a mountain, starting a family, changing careers, learning to fly, moving to New York, signing your book, traveling to Italy, getting a degree, basking in the sun, holding your family close, raising a glass to toast a dream come true.

*Only those who will risk going too far
can possibly find out how far one can go.*

T. S. ELIOT

# EPILOGUE

As long days of swimming, camera flashes, and cheering crowds faded into distant memories, I moved back to Washington. Andy finally made it to New York and married Jessica in 2001. Together they started ANDHOW! Theater Company where he is writing and producing plays and working with the best directors — including his wife. John finished his Ph.D. and became an economics professor at Amherst College. Now, back in the D.C. area, he's about to marry his Jessica.

My dad continues to see patients at his busy allergy practice in Maryland — the Allergy and Asthma Clinic of North Bethesda. My mom tried unsuccessfully to retire her goddess title.

Nearly a year after our celebration in Baton Rouge, I expected my life to return to normal — whatever *normal* was. Living in the same city as my parents gave me an opportunity to spend time with them. Every Friday I joined my mom and dad for lunch at Pizzeria Paradiso. Each week I noticed my dad having more difficulty climbing the ten steps to the entrance of the restaurant and walking the short distance to a table. He was still using a cane and struggling even more to walk. Had my Swim really accomplished anything? I couldn't get MS out of my mind.

One day, Andy (in D.C. for a visit), my mom, and I reminisced.

"Can you imagine how much easier it would be to do another fundraiser?"

"We're so much smarter now. And just think of the contacts. Finding sponsors would be a breeze."

"Think of the press," my mom said with all the excitement of a true PR Goddess.

"So, Nick, what are you going to do next?" one of them jokingly asked.

With my shoulder still popping and occasionally aching, I knew anything swimming-related was out.

"I could do a bike ride." The words tumbled out of my mouth before they had a chance to connect with my brain.

Maybe my statement wouldn't have sounded so strange if I had ever been a cyclist or if my longest ride had been more than thirty-two miles. What was I thinking?

The Swim was supposed to be a one-time event and then I would go on with my life. Why was I saying I could do a bike ride? I had to face the fact that maybe this *was* going on with my life.

In 1998, my family and I started in earnest to plan a bike ride for the summer of 2000. We all believed the project would be different because we knew what we were doing. We would make this event bigger, better, and more visible than the Swim. And it would be easier. We proved our naiveté has no bounds.

In our new venture, Dave — this time with Judy by his side — traveled behind me in an RV keeping me safe, once again. While John devised an effective and innovative fundraising plan for the Web site, Andy helped with logistics before joining me for five weeks on the road. My dad resumed his duties as our travel agent and, of course, my mom, amongst everything else, reclaimed her goddess title.

# EPILOGUE

In August 2000, I successfully completed a five-month, 10,000-mile bike loop around the perimeter of the United States — *Going the Distance: The Nationwide MS Bike Tour*. But then — that's another story.

Now, having completed *two* incredible events, I'm sharing my experiences and the lessons I've learned by speaking to audiences across the country.

Our efforts on behalf of MS continue through Going the Distance for MS Research, Inc. (www.goingthedistance.net)

# ACKNOWLEDGMENTS

Any dream can come true with the love and support of a great team. I give my sincere thanks to each of you who made this book possible.

To my mom, Connie Irons, the best co-author anyone could ever want. She made *Swim Lessons* what it is. I think there is another book (or two) in her.

To my dad, John Irons, reader extraordinaire, for his editorial suggestions. I appreciate his attention to the commas, periods, spelling, and spaces that I tend to ignore.

To my brothers, John and Andy, whose early insights on the manuscript helped bring this book to life.

To Jessica Davis Irons and Jessica Jones, who bring joy to my brothers' lives and have added a fun, new dimension to our family.

To my agents, Jonathon Lazear and Christi Cardenas, who believed in the book and were as eager as I was to see it in print.

To my editor, Eric Vrooman, who turned me into the writer I never knew I could be.

To Carl Lavin, whose suggestions on the manuscript made a world of difference.

To my designer, Sharon Thorpe, whose creative mind and artistic ability made me look great — again.

I also extend my heartfelt thanks to those who believed in the Mississippi Swim for Multiple Sclerosis and gave so much to make it happen.

To my mom, the PR goddess, whose dedication and countless hours of work can't be measured. I'm indebted to her for the success of the Swim.

To my dad, who is always there for me. He inspired me to swim 1,550 miles down a polluted river. What more needs to be said?

To my brother, Andy, who kept me happy, safe, and sane during the Swim. I would never have made it without him. ANDHOW!

To my brother, John, whose practical and innovative contributions lifted the project to the next level.

To my extended family: my grandparents Jack and Audrey Irons; my Aunt Lynn, Uncle Nick, and cousins Mike and Kiki Holman; and my Great-Aunt Babe. They were always there to cheer me on.

To Dave and Judy Douglas, who will always be like family to me.

To Dave and Judy's children and grandchildren, who shared Dave with us for two months.

To friends and members of the Boston College Swim Team — especially Andres Benach, Bob Yap, and Tyler Zenner. With their help, I never lost my love of swimming.

To Lance Jenson and the United States Power Squadrons escorts who kept us safe for more than four months.

To the United States Coast Guard Auxiliary escorts who filled in the gaps very nicely.

To Clay Evans, Bonnie Adair, and the members of Southern California Aquatics who prepared me for the swim.

To Susan Lemmon, Mary Brooks, Ann Cochran, and Cindy Moses, who helped make sense out of our logistical nightmare.

To Pat Ricks and his family and friends, who planned one of the best fundraisers anyone could hope for.

ACKNOWLEDGEMENTS

To the LSU swim team, the LSU band, Catfish Town, Baton Rouge Convention & Visitors Bureau, and Brian Spillman and the Louisiana Department of Wildlife and Fisheries for providing a wonderful welcome for us in Baton Rouge.

To Biogen, Inc., which contributed moral support to the Swim, financial support to MS research, and which has made a difference in my dad's life and in the lives of so many living with MS.

To our corporate sponsors, who supplied everything necessary for our four-month journey down the River. Without the generosity of these hotels, motels, B&B's and inns, restaurants, marinas, boating goods stores, grocers, and corporations large and small, the *Mississippi Swim for Multiple Sclerosis* would still be just a dream.

To the many kind supporters who sold T-shirts; made a corporate or personal donation; or went out of their way to provide transportation, a bed, food, supplies, a laugh, or a boost.

To the members of the media who told our story. Special thanks to Good Morning America, Joe Krebs, Barbara Harrison, Doug McElway, Susan Kidd, WRC-TV, Paul Levy, the Minneapolis Star Tribune, Griff Jenkins and Oliver North, Paul Harris, People, The Washington Post, the L.A. Times, AP newswire, AP radio, NPR, Kari Lydersen, Jim Galewski, Cary J. Hahn, Matt and Homey, Dave Lee, and WCCO Radio. MS families everywhere were the beneficiaries of their efforts.

To friends who supported my efforts, many of whom traveled miles to cheer me on: Hilary and Randy Wilkin, Jan and Jim McKenna, Laurie and Fred Levy, Kristi and Dick Yore, Marca and Bob Floyd, Debby and Jimmy Goodman, Suzie and Bryan Williams, Mona Benach, Ken Keen and Fiona Hill, Susan Lemmon, Joe Lagomarcino, Jon and Jed Redwine, Cindy and Bob Moses, Chris Tarantola, Cheryl Dahle, Ann and Chuck Cochran, Clayton Ruebensaal, Steve Skarky, Rob and David Walker, Paul Johnson, Bruce Johnson, the Bethesda BNI group, Donna Quick, Anita Barretto, Helene Hemus, and the loyal patients of the Allergy and Asthma Clinic of North Bethesda. I always knew they were behind me.

Finally, to everyone who is working on a daily basis to make a difference in the lives of those with MS, including the National MS Society, the Nancy Davis Foundation, the Paralyzed Veterans of America, Destination Cure, and Going the Distance for MS Research, Inc. We will find a cure.

Even with all the people who are mentioned here, there are many others, whom I love and appreciate, who are not. I hope you know who you are.

# APPENDIX A
## Making a Dream Come True

### A COMPELLING IDEA

**I Could Do Anything If I Only Knew What It Was: How to Discover What You Really Want and How to Get It**
By Barbara Sher with Barbara Smith
Published by DTP in 1995.

If you're having a hard time finding your compelling idea, *I Could Do Anything* may help. The simple exercises and sound advice will stimulate the discovery process.

**Wake-Up Calls: Making the Most Out of Every Day (Regardless of What Life Throws You)**
By Joan Lunden
Published by McGraw-Hill/Contemporary Books in 2001.

A collection of Joan Lunden's favorite anecdotes, quotations, and common sense wisdom; great strategies for everyday life.

### WRITE YOUR DREAM

**Bird by Bird**
By Anne Lamott
Published by Anchor in 1995.

Anne Lamott helps you find your voice and write with passion. Wise and wonderful — a good read.

**Writing Down the Bones: Freeing the Writer Within**
By Natalie Goldberg
Published by Shambhala Publications in 1986.

*Writing Down the Bones* uses anecdotes and fun exercises to make the process of writing easier and more meaningful for anyone.

## MAKE A PLAN

### Getting Results For Dummies®
By Mark H. McCormack
Published by John Wiley & Sons in 2000.

Another great *Dummies* book. This one can organize the most unorganized person. It will help you stay focused and achieve more than you ever thought possible.

### Time Management
By Marshall J. Cook
Published by Adams Media Corporation in 1998.

*Time Management* is another great book for those organizationally challenged among us. Interesting strategies for planning, filing, and general time management.

### Time Management for the Creative Person
By Lee T. Silber
Published by Three Rivers Press in 1998.

Finally!! A book on organization geared toward right-brained people. Before moving on to larger time-management issues, Silber starts with the basics — how to avoid losing your car keys. Brilliant.

## HAVE FUN

### Oh, the Things I Know!
### A Guide to Success, or, Failing That, Happiness
By Al Franken
Published by Dutton in 2002.

A hilarious parody of self-help books. Chapter titles include: "Oh, the Weight You Will Gain!"; "Oh, the Mistakes You'll Keep Repeating!"; and "Oh, What Doesn't Kill You Can Have Lingering Aftereffects!"

APPENDIX A

*The Polar Bear Waltz and Other Moments of Epic Silliness: Comic Classics from Outside Magazine's "Parting Shots"*
Outside Magazine (editor)
Published by W.W. Norton & Company in 2002.
A coffee-table book of oddball photographs from Outside Magazine. These sixty-seven full-color photos, featuring animals and humans, are sure to make you smile.

## ADJUST YOUR GOALS

*Procrastination: Why You Do It, What to Do About It*
By Jane B. Burka, Ph.D. and Lenora M. Yuen, Ph.D.
Published by Perseus Publishing in 1990.
Procrastination includes an excellent chapter on goal setting. It illustrates well the idea of breaking goals into smaller pieces.

## MOTIVATION

*It's Not Over 'Til It's Over*
By Al Silverman
Published by The Overlook Press in 2002.
Al Silverman recounts thirteen memorable sports comebacks. Just when you thought it was over, remarkable athletes turn the tide.

*Raising the Bar: New Horizons in Disability Sports*
By Artemis Joukowsky and Larry Rothstein
Published by Umbrage Editions, Inc. in 2002.
Raising the Bar compiles beautiful photography from disability sports events. It features interviews with some of the world's best disabled athletes. Truly inspirational.

## SELF-CONFIDENCE

### Feel the Fear and Do It Anyway
By Susan Jeffers, Ph.D.
Published by Fawcett Books in 1992.

*Feel the Fear and Do It Anyway* guides you in dealing with fear — a natural occurrence in everyone's life. Dr. Jeffers makes facing fear fun.

### Personal History
By Katharine Graham
Published by Vintage Books in 1998.

This autobiography of Katharine Graham, the force behind *The Washington Post*, is an amazing account of emerging self-esteem.

### Esteemable Acts: 10 Actions for Building Real Self-Esteem
By Francine Ward
Published by Broadway Books in 2003.

Francine Ward's book is based on the premise that self-esteem is built by taking action. This remarkable woman's life proves this theory.

## A GREAT TEAM

### Championship Team Building: What Every Coach Needs to Know to Build a Motivated, Committed & Cohesive Team
By Jeff Janssen
Published by Winning The Mental Game in 2002.

Written specifically for coaches, this book provides dozens of strategies for building a championship team. The concepts presented will work in sports, at the office, and in life.

### Winning the Mental Way: A Practical Guide to Team Building and Mental Training
By Karlene Sugarman, M.A.
Published by Step Up Publishing in 1999.

Learn to enhance the mental skills you'll need for a better performance in sports or in life.

# FLEXIBILITY

**How to Think Like Einstein: Simple Ways to Break the Rules and Discover Your Hidden Genius**
By Scott Thorpe
Published by Sourcebooks, Inc. in 2000.
Using Einstein as a model, Scott Thorpe convinces the reader that breaking the rules is the key that unlocks the hidden genius in all of us.

**Who Moved My Cheese? An A-Mazing Way to Deal with Change in Your Work and in Your Life**
By Spencer Johnson, M.D.
Published by Putnam in 1998.
Who Moved My Cheese? is a parable perfect for those who are facing a change, wanting a change, or afraid of a change in their life. A fast, easy read with a poignant message.

# CREATIVITY

**A Whack on the Side of the Head: How You Can Be More Creative**
By Roger Von Oech, Ph.D.
Published by Warner Books in 1998.
Von Oech has produced a lively book filled with games and fun exercises to help you break habitual thought patterns that inhibit creativity.

**Expect the Unexpected or You Won't Find It: A Creativity Tool Based on the Ancient Wisdom of Heraclitus**
By Roger Von Oech, Ph.D.
Published by Berrett-Koehler Publishing in 2002.
This follow-up to A Whack on the Side of the Head starts with the premise: "Creative thinking involves imagining familiar things in a new light, digging below the surface to find previously undetected patterns, and finding connections among unrelated phenomena." This fun book gives you practice in thinking creatively.

# APPENDIX B
## Multiple Sclerosis Web Sites

**MEDLINE Plus** *http://www.nlm.nih.gov/medlineplus*
A consumer resource provided by the National Institutes of Health that provides access to extensive information about multiple sclerosis and its treatments. It includes spellings and definitions of medical terms, generic and brand name drug information, and doctor locations and credentials.

**The Consortioum of MS Centers** *http://www.mscare.org*
A site primarily aimed at medical professionals, but containing some very useful information for people with MS.

**National MS Society** *http://www.nmss.org*
A resource for individuals with MS and their families that provides information pertaining to living with MS: MS treatments, scientific progress, publications and the Society's organization, structure, and functions. Provides information about MS specialty centers, ongoing basic and clinical research, MS Society publications for professionals, funding opportunities for research, and an annotated bibliography for health-care professionals.

# APPENDIX C
## Mississippi River

**The Mississippi and the Making of a Nation:**
**From the Louisiana Purchase to Today**
   By Stephen E. Ambrose, Sam Abell and Douglas G. Brinkley
   Published by National Geographic in 2002.
A full, rich history of the Mississippi River. Filled with Sam Abell's brilliant photography and Steven Ambrose's insights, this book is a great way to get to know the Big Muddy.

**The River We Have Wrought: A History of the Upper Mississippi**
   By John O. Anfinson
   Published by University of Minnesota Press in 2003.
A comprehensive history of the lock and dam system of the Mississippi River. *The River We Have Wrought* discusses the impact of politics on economics, the environment, and life along the Mississippi.

**Mississippi Solo: A River Quest**
   By Eddy L. Harris
   Published by The Lyons Press in 1999.
Eddy Harris shares the story of his solo canoe trip down the Mississippi. An inspiring travel narrative filled with stories of his encounters with people along the way.

**Upper Mississippi River Navigational Charts**
   Published by the U.S. Army Corps of Engineers in 1998.
   To purchase: Mississippi River Visitor Center (309) 794-5338.

***Lower Mississippi River Navigational Charts***
Published by the U.S. Army Corps of Engineers in 1994.
To purchase: U.S. Army Corps of Engineers Vicksburg Office (601) 631-5042.

***Quimby's 2002 Cruising Guide: The Complete Listing of Marinas and Locks on the Inland and Gulf Intracostal Waterways.***
Published by The Waterways Journal, Inc. in 2002.
The ultimate guide to boating along the Mississippi River. It provides lock and dam information, marina locations, and fun facts about each section of the river.

# APPENDIX D
## Swimming

**Total Immersion: The Revolutionary Way to Swim Better, Faster, and Easier**
By Terry Laughlin with John Delves
Published by Fireside in 1996.
In *Total Immersion*, Terry Laughlin shows how to swim smoothly and more efficiently. An excellent book for anyone interested in increasing the distance covered by each stroke.

**Swimming into the 21st Century**
By Cecil M. Colwin
Published by Human Kinetics in April 1993.
This book details the latest in swimming technique. All four strokes, starts, and turns are included.

**Swimming Even Faster**
By Ernest W. Maglischo
Published by McGraw-Hill in 1993.
If you have ever wondered what makes a swimmer fast, this 755-page book is for you. It is very technical on the mechanics of competitive swimming, training, and racing. An amazing wealth of knowledge.

**Swimming Drills for Every Stroke**
By Ruben J. Guzman
Published by Human Kinetics in 1998.
Improve your swimming by doing stroke drills. In this book, Guzman shows you ninety-one different drills.

**Gold in the Water: The True Story of Ordinary Men and Their Extraordinary Dream of Olympic Glory**
By P. H. Mullen Jr.
Published by St. Martin's Press in 2001.
A book focusing on two swimmers training for the 2000 Olympics in Sydney, Australia. A powerful account of the daily training of elite-level swimmers.

# About the Authors

Nick Irons is an author, ultra-endurance athlete, entrepreneur and a dreamer. He was the second person in history to swim the Mississippi River and the first to do it with the locks and dams of its modern form. He lives in Bethesda, MD.

Connie Irons is Nick's mom. She is also a major contributor to this book, resident PR expert, and part of the family dream team behind this extraordinary adventure.

Made in the USA
Middletown, DE
30 May 2019